Stories of Limerick

By Denis O'Shaughnessy

Previous publications:

A Spot So Fair, 1998

The Pig Buyer and the Pope, 1999

Limerick: 100 Stories of the Century, 2000

How's Your Father? 2002

The Bus Excursion, 2004

Published by Margopress, 2006.
12 Janemount Park, Limerick. 061-346662.

Printed by Ryan Printers Ltd.

Front picture: The great Todds fire of 1959.
Back: Lord Aberdeen parades before opening Limerick's Great Exhibition of 1906.

Foreword

ONE of the great pleasures of the Christmas season is the appearance of yet another book on Limerick by Denis O'Shaughnessy. He has not failed us this year, producing yet another wide-ranging, well researched and entertaining volume covering a wide range of forgotten and lesser-known stories about a city he loves so well.

Previous works by Denis have in the main quickly sold out and become collectors' items. His secret is his revelations of local social history which you will not find in heavier tomes, many of which when bought are left largely unread on bookshelves.

His latest offering, *Stories of Limerick*, is yet another wide-ranging, well researched and entertaining volume. Did you know, for instance, that Limerick could have surpassed Knock or even Lourdes if the apparition of Our Lady in the Mount Convent in 1880 had the benefit of a good PRO agency, or was witnessed by the nuns rather than the orphans? One of his main stories is that of the Todds inferno of 1959 which resulted in the main shopping block of the city centre being razed to the ground. Denis also reveals the first fully researched story of the most infamous instance of cannibalism at sea that took place on *The Francis Spaight* bound for Limerick in 1835.

These are just appetisers. There are twenty-six stories in all ranging from famous local myths, including the appearance of the cloven-hoofed devilish dancer in the Stella Ballroom, a story which had vibrations even to the far ends of the county as I can recall from my childhood in West Limerick in the 1950's. By all accounts he was a charming hoofer, seemingly treating the favoured ladies with more respect than they had been accustomed to from the average Limerick man at the time.

A notable feature of all the author's books is his ability to draw stories from local characters. Thus, you will fall about the place reading of the exploits of the legendary Michael Crowe, and the army adventures of Joe Neiland in the years of World War II, popularly known as the Emergency. Newspapers, too, are great source material of his, and he has the knack of turning up quirky articles and following them through until another absorbing story is revealed.

Denis is also adept at focussing on items of social history which were of major importance in people's lives. These rarely feature in standard history works, and have either vanished entirely or are about to disappear. One example is the once highly popular Limerick card game of '45,' which some maintain, as the younger generation lose interest, will eventually die out. He writes from experience of the game and its history, and of the sheer magic of the arrival of parcels from America to the family home in the Sandmall.

Limerick people, both at home and especially abroad, are in debt to the author for the contribution he has made in recording important facets of the city's social history. His books have given us great pleasure over the years, are liberally quoted from, and indeed pass through more than one set of hands. No greater compliment can be paid to a writer.

-LIAM IRWIN

Contents

The Boodeyman, Devil in the Stella, and other local myths

This 1950's photograph of the Stella Ballroom shows a statute of the Blessed Virgin looming large over the bandstand, the only ballroom in the country reputed to have such a religious display. In all probability the statue was erected in the honour of the Marian Year, 1954, but some maintain it was put in place following the rumour that swept town that a cloven footed dancer made his appearance there a year or two earlier on.

THE Stella Ballroom was a popular rendezvous for local dancers, its heyday being the 1950's and 60's during the showband era. One Saturday night, in the early '50's, a handsome looking man asked this girl to dance and she duly obliged. Debonair, and a splendid dancer and charmer to boot, the young lady was sure she was going to click as, when the dance finished, the dark haired stranger invited her to partake of refreshments in the mineral bar. She gladly acquiesced but suddenly fainted. Revived by her friends, she told them that whatever way she looked down, she saw that the stranger had cloven feet. He was of course, nowhere to be seen. It was the devil she was dancing with and the story swept the city the following days, its authenticity being believed wholesale.

The incident was high on the agenda in conversations for a long time, and the rumour spread that a well known Franciscan was called in to bless the hall. Later on a statute of Our Lady was erected in the ballroom, generally believed to honour the Marian Year of 1954, but others liked to believe it was erected to discourage further visits of the Evil One! One of the many myths that has sprung up over the years in Limerick. Then there was the Mystery Man. A few years before the devil's appearance in the Stella, rumour spread like wildfire that a Mystery Man had arrived in the city. No one seemed to know who he was, or what he was up to, or even what he looked like.

Yet, there were those who swore they saw him. He was seen in Janesboro one night, in Killeely the next, and word had it that a woman fainted in the Island Field when she saw him looking in the window! All it needed was for someone to say "I saw the Mystery Man" and they were the centre of attention.

The Mystery Man was never caught. But why should he be? He was never reported for having committed a crime, never interfered with anyone. Some said he was a figment of the imagination, but others said yes, there really was such thing as the Mystery Man.

We musn't forget the Boody Man. Possibly a relation of the Mystery Man, he was first seen through a window on a dark night by a woman in Prospect and the sighting caused great consternation. There was even a parody to the air of the popular song, *Bless This House: Bless this house, to God we pray, from the Boody Man save us this day.*

When we were young, there were several myths doing the rounds connected with the mortuary in St Mary's Church. One of the most popular was that one night, after the removal of a corpse to the mortuary (or dead house as it was known then), a woman was inadvertently locked in. When the parish clerk, Willie Bartlett, opened up the next morning he found her with all her hair pulled out and she frothing at the mouth. She wound up in the mental home.

On the morning of another funeral the coffin was opened to give a girl who had come from England a chance to see her father for the last time, and to say her final goodbye. To the family's horror, when the coffin was opened, the white lace on the inside of the coffin was covered in blood and the corpse's fingernails were scratched to the bone.

St Thomas' Island in Corbally in our youth was a magical place to explore, with its castle at one end and the ruins of the red-bricked mansion once owned by the Tuthall family at the other end. In the middle of the ruins, was the entrance to a cellar which legend had it contained a secret passage going all the way under the river and coming out at a secret spot in St Mary's Cathedral. The fact that the tunnel, reputed to be used by the Dominicans (who had a monastery on the island in the middle ages), was blocked, added more mystery to the myth, or legend. Needless to say we never found the tunnel, or did anybody else as far as I know.

Then there are the modern myths. Some years ago, a couple living in the city suburbs woke up to find their car had been stolen during the night. They duly reported the robbery to the Guards and to their pleasant surprise, the car was found next morning in the county, without a scratch on it. An envelope left in the front seat contained an anonymous note of apology from the perpetrator who explained that as a matter of extreme urgency he had to borrow the car. To the couple's delight, the envelope also contained a pair of tickets for the Bunratty Medieval Banquet the following Saturday night, as an act of atonement.

The couple duly attended the banquet, enjoyed themselves immensely, and when they came home found that their house had been completely cleaned out!

A farmer on the Limerick/Cork border watched with interest as the gas pipeline from Kinsale was being laid on the periphery of his lands. Half joking, half serious, he said to one of the workmen one day wouldn't it be gas if he could be connected to the supply on the quiet. The workman said why not and after £600 changed hands he was duly connected. The farmer's delight turned to alarm when after about a month the supply dried up and thinking there might be a leak, traced the pipes through his lands. There was no leak, just a large

Stepen O'Gorman's sketch of the sea monster in the Limerick Docks in 1922.

Kosangas cylinder connected by pipe underneath the ground!

On a weekend some time back, a local woman bought an expensive dress in one the city's better known boutiques. She returned the dress a few days later with apologies, claiming she had second thoughts, and then asked to know if she could be reimbursed. She was refused. She had worn the dress to a function at the weekend and the proprietor had spotted her in a photograph in one of the local newspapers!

The Park district, noted market garden area in days gone by, was populated by extremely hard working families who were reputed to be direct descendants of the Danes, founders of the city. The dark, sallow complexions and generally small stature of the Parkmen used be pointed out as evidence of their descendancy. The myth, however, has been scoffed at by historians who claim that the family names of the Park people, such as the predominant McNamara and Clancy families, straight away debunk such theories.

Another myth about the Vikings was that it was they built the Abbey River, thus making an island fortress of their settlement based in the area now known as Merchants' Quay. Thus it became known as Inis Siobtan, now known as King's Island. There is no evidence to suggest that the Vikings ever built the river, but neither is there evidence to prove that they didn't.

One of the greatest of all local myths is the alleged appearance of a Lough Ness type monster in the Docks area in 1922, the story of which we have written in "Limerick: One Hundred Stories of the Century." There was reputed to have been hundreds of witnesses and two, A. E. Aldridge, skipper of a schooner in the docks at the time, and local teenager, Stephen O'Gorman, were amongst them. They have recorded their impressions of the monster, both reports corroborating closely.

Captain Aldridge described the monster, as it passed his ship, as being large and black and shiny and about the size of a small submarine. It had a large long neck, about twelve feet long, held proudly erect and shaped like a swan's. It waved its small head from side to side and its bright shining eyes seemed to express alarm. Behind its long neck for a distance of ten or twelve feet was a massive black cone-shaped hump, which rose for a few feet out of the water, but no part of the creature's body could be seen between the hump and neck, this part being submerged.

Stephen O'Gorman, a teenager at the time, was playing handball in Shannon Street when he saw the crowds heading for the docks. He and his pals followed them and claimed he saw the monster, exactly as Captain Aldridge described it.

"The creature travelled as far as Sarsfield Bridge and then turned back. There were hundreds of people lining the quays and when the monster turned downstream, a group of Free State soldiers from the Strand Barracks started to fire at it until the creature passed Barrington's Pier and disappeared into the distance. They did not hit it, merely content to hit the water behind it. I believe they were just trying to encourage it on its way." Stephen emigrated to England and people would smile when he'd relate the story. However, when Captain Aldridge wrote to the Leader in 1974 looking for corroboration of his story, Stephen was delighted to do so, and stated: "now it is my turn to smile."

Corbally's Joe Neiland, and many other Limerickmen, took part in what was the greatest turn-out of an Irish army in the history of the State when on September 13th, 1942, 20,000 troops paraded through the centre of Cork following manoeuvres between the 1st and 2nd Divisions. They were joined by units of the 7th Brigade, Southern Command, of which Joe and many other Limerickmen were members.
(Hanley Collection)

The invisible truck: Joe's Neiland's stories of the Emergency

In 1941, as Europe was in the middle of the greatest conflict it had ever known, and as Japan was laying its final plans for its act of infamy in Pearl Harbour, the threat of invasion to this country was very real. Even though neutrality had been declared, no one knew from one day to the next whether England, her convoys being decimated by German U-Boats in the Atlantic, would attempt to take back our ports, which had been handed over by Churchill some years previously. Or whether Adolf Hitler would invade and use this country as a platform from which to invade England.

Conscious of these threats, Taoiseach Eamonn de Valera made regular and emotional appeals to the young men of Ireland to join the armed forces to defend their land in its hour of need. His pleas were heeded, and all over the country, thousands of young men answered the call, army barracks being inundated with recruits joining up to protect their fair land.

Sarsfield Barracks was no exception and many of these answering the call hailed from St Mary's, a parish inured to warfare, and whose forebears defended the walls in sieges, died in the trenches of Flanders, and in the 1930's fought on the dusty plains of Spain to oust the Socialist regime.

Amongst them was the hero of this story, one Joe Neiland from Bishop Street, a stripling young lad who at the tender age of sixteen decided his country needed him, as Kitchener once asked of the young men of England.

Like a young lad calling his pal to come out for a game of football, Joe knocked at the door of his friend Mick Fahy to know if he'd accompany him in this great adventure. Alas, Mick's mother was within hearing range and banged the door in Joe's face telling him to get lost. Undaunted, the would-be recruit headed for Sarsfield Barracks on his own, flinging his school-books over Mathew Bridge on the way. It was an act which in its finality showed the single-mindedness of the now redundant schoolboy.

Joining other recruits at the gates of the barracks, he was soon admitted, but told to wait as the guard was being mounted to the strains of "The Little Three Leaved Shamrock of Glenrose," played by the army band. Having passed his medical, Joe was allowed to go home to make final arrangements and say his goodbyes, and told to return in the afternoon. On the way out he was stopped by two of his fellow enlisted parishioners, formidable Garryowen rugby players Brendan Morgan and Sean McNamara, their homely advice to him consisting of "go home you young fool you, Neiland."

Back in the homestead, his father, surprisingly, made no attempt to stop him joining up, warning him it was on his own head and not to expect to be baled out in a week or two when the novelty wore off. Word was out on the street that Joe was off to defend his country and the house filled up with well-wishers, many of whom would have dropped in out of curiosity.

Across the road, the nuns of the Mercy Convent, who though mostly enclosed, had great access to happenings in the parish, sent over a parcel to the young recruit containing a pair of blessed scapulars, a rosary beads, several religious tracts and two packages of twenty Sweet Afton cigarettes. Two maiden aunts of the Hayes family who had a shop in Nicholas Street, gave Joe a note to give to their brother, a sergeant in Cork, where the new recruit was now bound. The note told all about Joe, where he was from, and to look out for him.

Transported to Cork, they were not long in Collins Barracks when the bugle sounded and being unacquainted with the routine, the new boys were slow in answering its call. The door burst open and a sergeant in language that Joe was unaccustomed to, upbraided them in the most violent manner possible. He was to learn that this was the brother of the Hayes aunts, and he duly tore up the note.

They were now fitted out in regulation gear and to say these were assorted is to put it mildly. Joe was given a Vickers helmet, modelled on the Nazi style (which became outmoded shortly afterwards), a stiff collar tunic, the sleeves of which stopped half way down his arms; pants, leggings, boots, and a great-coat. A schoolmate who had also joined up, Tommy Dodd from the Island Road, being diminutive in size, his great-coat was much too long and trailed along the ground.

Sporting these ill-fitting uniforms, they were marched to Glanmire Station, and Joe remembered the sniggering of the Cork people as they marched past. They were bound for Croom, one of the three County Limerick outposts (the others were Bruree and Ballinagarde House of "I doubt it says Croker" fame) and our hero's life in the army was now officially under way. He was to have many adventures and be part of many hilarious situations for the remainder of the Emergency, as it was then called here.

He was now a fully fledged member of the grandly named No. 5 Platoon B Company 9th Desmond Infantry Batt 7th Brigade Southern Command. Their Commander was Colonel Thomas Feely, a man of great physical strength. whom Joe described as a natural leader and a great character to boot. Under "Old Tom's" command, as he was affectionately known, the Brigade, despite serious shortages of artillery, was whipped into shape and programmed to put into effect contingency plans to foil the enemy.

Joe remembers when they were down to one tank. "It got the kid gloves treatment, and was transported by low loader in case anything happened it."

One of the big problems of army transport was the lack of petrol, which led to a hilarious charade. If there was no trucks for manoeuvres, the motions still had to be gone through. According to Joe, when the sergeant called "de-truck" the troops had to make-believe they were descending from the lorry, lifting their legs and doing the appropriate actions, and at the end of the day when "on-truck" was called, they had to pretend they were climbing back on.

While life was no picnic at times, with regular route marches of up to twelve miles, the grub, Joe recalled, was on the whole, pretty good. While civilians were now feeling the full rigours of the rationing system, only the best was good enough for our boys who at any moment could be called to spill their life's blood for their country.

"Breakfast generally consisted of rasher, egg, sausage, black and white pudding, and quarter loaf of bread. There was regular roast beef, veg. and potato for dinner, and being exempt from religious restrictions, there was even stews on days of abstinence," Joe recalled.

Then there was the skulduggery regarding provisions, especially tea, the scarcest of commodities. "I remember being poured a mug of tea one evening, it had an obnoxious taste, like as if old socks had been dipped into it. One of the men complained, the cook summoned the Orderly, who on tasting the tea, declared it to be perfect and told the complainant gruffly to carry on! I saw a rather stout cook being halted one day and when ordered to open his great-coat a pile of provisions fell to the ground! When we did a stint in Sarsfield Barracks we were put guarding the coal, piled up against the walls. It was a regular thing to throw some into the adjoining back yards of some of the very grateful people in Wolfe Tone Street."

Several Limerickmen, members of the 7th Brigade, are included in this photograph of the Emergency years, taken in 1944 following a training session in preparation for the Munster Senior Rugby Cup. The Brigade won the All-Ireland Army championship the previous season, but were beaten in the replay of the Munster Senior Cup Final the following year by Dolphin. Front row, left, Paddy Griffin, Ger (Spot) O'Donovan, Brendan Morgan and Paddy Carr, with, behind them, Dave Ringrose, Sean McNamara.

Sometimes, a general purgative (laxative) was issued by the medical corps and put into the soldier's tea. "It was deadly," recalled Joe. "It was dubbed a No. 9, why I don't know, and when it took effect you literally dropped everything."

Wages for the troops were thirteen shillings a week, and there would be stoppages out of that. "The serious stoppages came if by chance you fell out of a route march. You were fined heavily for doing so, it was a sort of disciplinary punishment."

Joe's outstanding memory of Croom was the night it was nearly blown up. An NCO had been charged with stealing a revolver, and under open arrest with a fellow NCO guarding him, they both managed to get drunk. They raided the magazine and put a mine under it and blew it up. Windows were broken all over the village and the roof of the church was damaged, debris was scattered as far as Carass.

"Confusion reigned supreme and word went out that we were being attacked from the air," recalled Joe. "Guns were produced and rifles and bren guns were fired at the sky. A special unit was rushed out from Sarsfield Barracks and the NCO's got fifteen years each in jail."

Local installations that were guarded by the 7th Brigade were the Docks, and the power station at Ardnacrusha, where a concrete pillbox built for defence purposes can still be seen on the approach to the bridge (city side) over the Head Race.

Like tea, there was a huge shortage of cigarettes during the Emergency, and out of desperation soldiers often rolled turf dust in cigarette papers as a last resort.

"The results were horrendous," Joe recalled. "A supplier in Clare Street called Lucky Moore was in the way of getting cigarettes and knowing him I was often sent in for supplies. I was usually successful. I often cycled but one day when walking in I was overtaken by this motor car and the driver shouted to hop in as he couldn't stop. The car, with some sort of a balloon at the back, was being driven by gas generated by a fire, and I was as black as a Darkie Minstrel when I got to Limerick."

Then there was the famous route march from Bruree to Glenbeigh in Co.Kerry which took five days. Driven by truck, the army pipe band went ahead of the march, waited at the outskirts of important towns, and when the troops arrived the band led the march triumphantly

A welcome break for a mug of tea and a sandwich during Emergency manoeuvres. Note armbands on left arms to facilitate umpires identifying opposing forces.
(Hanley Collection)

through the streets. Badly blistered feet was the most common problems on route marches.

"There was manoeuvres in Co. Cork, and several soldiers were drowned crossing the Blackwater and Bride Rivers. If your platoon was captured, your kit, including your food, was taken from you, but farmers particularly were generous, no one ever starved," Joe maintained. Following those manoeuvres, they marched in one of the biggest military parades ever seen in the country, when joining the 1st and 2nd Divisions, they marched eight abreast through the centre of Cork City on September 13th, 1942.

While Ireland, to the world, appeared to be strictly neutral, Joe maintained that this was not so. "I saw members of the British Imperial staff observing manoeuvres with their Irish counterparts, and English planes which crashed-landed were loaded on low loaders to be taken to Northern Ireland. We guarded a German plane shot down in Co. Cork and the crew was interred in the Curragh, while those from the British plane were spirited back to the North. "

Rugby was very popular in the Southern Command and they saw some great matches. "Many of the Garryowen legends were in action such as Sean McNamara, Brendan Morgan, Mossy Curtin, Dave Ringrose, and Paddy Griffin, who in his officer's uniform was as handsome a man as you saw in the army."

Many of the more adventurous young soldiers yearned for action and deserted to England to take part in the European theatre. Superior pay was a big draw too. "Several asked me to go but I desisted. Most of them were promoted promptly thanks to the training they got here. I met some of them in later years and they did very well for themselves, such as those who volunteered for Palestine after the war and wound up with fine pensions."

Joe had several postings, the most unique being Valentia Island in Co. Kerry where they guarded the cable link. "As it was across water, it was treated as foreign service, and you were credited with this, with extra pay!

"We were billeted at one stage in Ballinagarde House in Ballyneety where the famous Croker family lived. The gardens were full of Greek god style statues and on a few occasions shots were fired at them, sentries in the dark taking them for intruders. I was on duty one night and the moon suddenly came out and what I could swear was a ghost appeared in front of me and I dropped my rifle and ran. It turned out it was a bronze statute of a nude, and I was lucky I wasn't shot for desertion. There was a mysterious, musky odour in the house during the night and all attempts to trace it were unsuccessful. Strangely, it disappeared during the day."

Air defences were minimal, with just a handful of anti-aircraft guns in the country, the rifle was to be used against low flying aircraft! The handful of corvettes were also poorly armed and troops were used to shoot at sea mines with their rifles.

How would they have done if the country was invaded? "With such poor equipment we could only have hoped for a staying period, that's why we were trained in guerrilla warfare."

How did they manage for entertainment during those years? "There were some great singers around, and you were never short of laughs with the all the characters."

Joe, who went on to become one of the leading bass-baritones with the Limerick and Choral Operatic Society, only discovered he could sing when he joined the army.

"I was thrown out of the choir in Quay Lane School by a Brother nicknamed Monkey Callaghan. He said I was a crow and when they won in the Feis they were taken to Killaloe as a treat and I was left behind. At a sing-song in Croom one night I was asked to sing and surprised myself when I rendered 'Alice Blue Gown' with favourable results."

Would he have done the same thing all over again?

"Certainly. It was one of the greatest experiences of my life. It was tough at times, but the comradeship, the laughs, the characters, made it all worth while. You could say I went in as a boy and came out as a man."

He was in Cork in recent years and saw a group of Ex-Servicemen in the lobby of the hotel he was staying in. He approached and asked if any of his old buddies in the No. 5 Platoon during the Emergency were around. "Not at all sir, they're all dead a long time."

Except for our Joe, who hail and hearty has his foot well on the ladder of his eightieth decade, and whose appetite for and interest in life is as great as it was in those far-off days when he joined up to defend his country against the threat of invasion by the great powers.

Joe Neiland (right), bass-baritone, starring in the Limerick Choral and Operatic Society's production of 'Maritana', City Theatre, 1958, with tenor Gerald Davies.

Were you there in 1978 when Munster beat the All-Blacks? If you are in any of the above photographs it will be proof identity of your presence, not like the many thousands who claim to have been there and cannot prove it.

Mistaken identity and other rugby stories

Garryowen, winners of the Munster Senior Cup, 1951-52. Back row: Tom Reid, Sean Healy, Jimmy Keyes, Richard (Dickie) Harris, Niall Quaid, Aengus McMorrow. 2nd row: Tom O'Loughlin, Pete Lawless, Billy Quaid, Jack Ryan, Gordon Wood, Paddy Lysaght, Sean McNamara, Sean O'Dea, Ned Waters. Seated: W. O'Connor, hon. treasurer; John Leahy, Willie Reid, Paddy Quilligan, Kevin Quilligan, capt.; Michael Quaid, President; Brendan Morgan, Tony O'Donovan, Joe Reid.

FOR Shannon RFC's Colm Tucker, 1980 was a memorable season in more ways than one. A replacement in the earlier part of the season against France in Paris, the Shannon man was famously named as "C. C. Fucker" in the match programme. An appellation that transcended all languages, and Parisians speculated mightily as to how anyone could be bestowed with such a wondrous name. Needless to say, the programme is now a valued collector's item, with Colm himself holding one.

It was an era when Irish selectors still played molly bawn with Limerick players and being a sub for the French match was the nearest Colm got to the Irish team that year. The Lions selectors, however, were more enlightened when naming him on the team to tour South Africa, and the Shannon man had an outstanding tour, playing some memorable matches and winning two test caps.

Rugby pundit George Hook, writing on the spirit of Munster rugby, credits Colm with a famous address to his Shannon team-mates about to take the field against Garryowen, the ancient enemy, in the Munster Cup: "There's only one ball, and if we hold on to it they can't win!"

Some years back, a group of Shannon supporters stopped at a pub in Buttevant on their way back from a match in Cork. It was of a Sunday, and they were warmly welcomed by the proprietoress who seemed delighted when told they had won their match. She put several plates of sandwiches in front of them and the lads thought that this was terrific form, demolishing the food as quick as you could say "Come on Shannon."

"What was the score?" the proprietoress enquired.

"15-9," was the reply.

"Good," she says. "and tell me, how did our John Murphy play?"

The lads looked at one another.

"Can't say we know anyone of that name on the team," one of the group volunteered.

Herself tu-tutted in exasperation.

"Of course you do, sure wasn't he playing left corner back"

It is not recorded what her reaction was when the local G.A.A. team trooped in later on.

The *Limerick Leader* of Saturday, November 29, 1952, carried a story of an un-named rugby player who, being dropped off his team, took it too much to heart. He went out and got blind drink, was arrested, and wound up in court. Interestingly, this was the height of an era when, depending who you were, your name could be kept out of newspaper reports of court cases, as was the hero of this little anecdote. There was also a practice in all sports reports that the names of those who were sent off the field for foul play were not published!

On with the story of the errant footballer of 1952: "A Limerick rugby player the other day heard that he had just been dropped from his team by the selection committee. 'He got drunk, thinking this new form of training would improve his chances,' said Mr. Dermot G. O'Donovan, solicitor, in today's District Court when the player was charged with public drunkenness.

"He played on a very representative team that day and he got word he had been dropped,' Mr. Donovan added.

"Justice Gleeson – Did he give the Guards any trouble?"

"Mr. O'Donovan – No. He obeyed the whistle all right."

Amid prolonged laughter, the Justice applied the Probation Act.

The 2nd World War Years, or the Emergency as it was known here, were times of great austerity, all kinds of items being extremely scarce and rationed. Money, needless to say, was as scarce as Ian Paisley saying yes.

The minute book of a committee meeting of Shannon R.F.C. on December 5th 1944, amply demonstrates this lack. A discussion arose as to how a team destined to play against Glenstal should travel to the match. Sean McNamara proposed, and Christy Quilligan seconded, that the club should use motor cars but that the hire of same should not cost more than £4. If cars not available for £4 or less, the team should cycle to Glenstal, a distance of eight miles.

An amendment was proposed by Alec McConkey, seconded by John Joe Cleary, that cars should not be hired, but that the team should cycle. The proposer said that the match was not important enough to warrant expenditure of £4, taking into consideration the financial position of the club.

Sadly, the secretary never recorded the outcome of the discussion.

In his playing days with Dublin's St. Mary's, New Zealander Brent Pope (famously sent off for downing Young Munster's Francis Brosnahan in the 1993 A.I.L final, and now a rugby broadcaster) was preparing with his team-mates to travel down to Limerick to play

Bohemians, winners of the Munster Senior Cup in 1959. Standing; Donal Holland, Jack Meaney, Billy Hurley, Maurice Walsh, Billy Slattery, Dom Dinneen, Caleb Powell, Brendan O'Dowd, Johnny Ryan, J. W. Stokes. Seated: Mick English, Christy English, Basil Fitzgibbon, Dermot Geary, capt., Paddy Moran, Paddy Downes, Paddy O'Callaghan. Front: Jimmy McGovern and Tom Cleary.

Young Munster in a League match. He spotted one of the trendy young players packing a pair of white football boots into his kit-bag. Alarm bells began to ring in Brent's head. Knowing the reputation of the Limerick crowd, and especially when they were playing in Greenfields (sometimes dubbed the Killing Fields), he advised the young buck to put his boots away, and wear the more conventional ones.

Greenfields was also humorously dubbed Gethsemane Park due to the famous incident when an eager Young Munster was alleged to have bitten the ear of a St. Mary's (Dublin) front row forward.

Then there was the yarn about Pako Fitzgerald and the Claw who were panned out after a particularly tough match one day in the Killing Fields.

Peter: "I can tell you Pako, here's a man with two very sore balls.'

Pako: 'You don't say Peter, whose are they?'

One of the great scenes in John Breen's splendid play *Alone it Stands*, is when the wife of the rugby fanatic, giving birth to twins, names them Garry and Owen, knowing full well her husband is a rabid anti-Garryowen man.

The late Willie Woodrow, of the Sandmall, and his wife Anne, went two better. Besides naming two of their sons Garry and Owen, they named the other two Liam and Rick!

Paul O'Connell was playing a stormer against Leinster, dominating the line-out and loose, tackling like a demon and scoring four tries into the bargain. Munster led 28-0 at half-time and Anthony Foley says the team may as well take a rest and let O'Connell play away on his own for the second half.

He met O'Connell that night and asked what was the final score.

'49-7' says O'Connell.

'What? You let that crowd in for a try?' exclaims Foley.

'I couldn't help it,' says O'Connell. 'I was in the sin bin at the time!'

The legendary Dodo Reddan, who demonstrated her loyalty to Young Munster by dressing up her dogs in the club colours and parading them in a pram to Thomond Park whenever there was a big match on. She was in Lansdowne Road with her four legged friends in 1993 when Young Munster won the All-Ireland League. Her dogs travelled up in the goods compartment of the train in company with the club mascot, a goat. A taxi driver spurned the chance of becoming part of the legend when refusing the goat's fare to Lansdowne Road: an obliging coal truck driver stepped in and did the needful.

When Our Lady appeared in Limerick

THE morning of Sunday, August 15th, 1880, was exceptionally sultry in Limerick City and it came as no surprise when the first of several thunder showers, with its attendant thunder, lightning and torrential rain, struck at lunch time and continued into the afternoon.

It was also the Feast Day of the Assumption of the Blessed Mary into Heaven, and the writer of the annals of the Sisters of Mercy noted that down in St Mary's Parish the feast was observed with due solemnity. None more so than in the mother house of the Sisters of Mercy in St Mary's Convent. and as the community assembled at 7 pm for final prayers, not much notice was taken of a messenger who had arrived from the branch house in Mount St Vincent with a note for the Reverend Mother.

Little did the assembly know that the contents of this note was to cause intense excitement throughout the city, country and abroad, and would become the subject of much conjecture in the leading newspaper of the age, the *London Times*, who sent over a reporter and photographer.

In an age when mortality rate, especially for mothers giving birth was very high, the amount of children left in care was substantial and Mount St Vincent was established especially by the Mercy Order to cater for the needs of these children. The orphanage at peak capacity, was able to cater for 180 girls.

On the Sunday in question, over one hundred of the orphans, used to the freedom of the open fields that then surrounded the orphanage in Mount Kennett, were kept indoors owing to the ferocity of the storms. About 5 o'clock in the afternoon, the storm began to abate and permission was given to about one hundred of the children to go outdoors and play.

Thunder could still be heard, but in the distance, and the children were told by their superior "not to fear if they heard further peals but to pray to the Blessed Virgin and that she would protect them."

They were not long in the playground when a lingering piece of thunder clapped extremely loudly and mindful of the admonition they had been given, instead of running back to the orphanage they prayed together, reciting the Litany of Loreto and all then joined in the singing of the hymn "Look Down O Mother Mary."

And Mary obeyed.

Suddenly one of the orphans cried "look at the sky, there is the Blessed Virgin." And there, to the astonishment and fear of the children, could be seen a vision of Our Lady attired in white, with a blue sash round and down from her waist, and a crown on her head. She held the Infant Saviour on her arm, with a Rosary beads drawn from the side which hung over to the other hand. An angel knelt at each side upholding a cloud of silvery light surrounding the Queen of Heaven.

The child who first cried out nearly fainted. Most of the children saw the apparition, but not all. They afterwards looked pale and agitated, and at the time felt almost spellbound with delight.

The apparition had taken place at a spot looking towards Henry Street over a clump of trees north of the convent. When the vision withdrew, the children continued their prayers and in about ten minutes she reappeared, this time in a line with the orphanage.

So absorbed were the children with the apparitions that none thought of telling the Sisters and it was about 5.40 when the startling accounts began to filter through to the community room.

The nuns rushed out to be greeted with a babble of voices and eventually when calming the children down and hearing of the vision, began to recite the Litany that they too might be favoured by the Celestial Vision.

A contemporary re-enactment of the apparition of Our Lady witnessed by orphans in Mount St. Vincent Convent, Mount Kennett, on Sunday 15th August, 1880. To the right is the front of the convent and the spire of the convent chapel. The children witnessing the apparition are playing in what was then an open field to the left of the orphanage. Drawn from photographs and sketches of the convent by W. Collins of Dublin.

There was to be no reappearance but one or two of the children said they saw figures representing Our Lord and Our Lady again, but these had disappeared when the throng diverted their gaze from the spot where Our Lady had first appeared.

Watch was kept into the night for a recurrence of the vision, and at dawn the next morning, but there were no further manifestations. The children spent most of the day praying without any repeat of the vision, and at length only a few lingered in the playground. One little girl said "let us kneel down and say three more Hail Mary's and maybe Holy Mary would come to us."

The prayers were scarcely ended when the Holy Virgin appeared, but not in any of the places seen before. The child fell back, quite overcome by the sight. It was then about half past five and the cries and agitation of the children having been heard by the Sisters in lecture, they hastened out. One only this time was to get a transient view of the Heavenly Being, just when the upper part of the figure was concealed partly by light fleece vapour, which did not permit discerning the expression of her countenance, yet the drapery and outstretched hands as represented in the Immaculate Conception looked so distinct that she could count the fingers, had the time being given.

On the Tuesday evening five of the orphans again beheld the Blessed Virgin, as if encircled by a bower of roses.

A visitor to the convent at this time was Miss Monsell, of the County Limerick ruling class family, who spoke to the children who had seen the vision, and was also shown the places from which the apparition was seen. Her mother, Lady Emly, visited some days after and she too was given a full account of the visions and the places from which they were seen.

The first, outside of the convent, to hear of the apparitions, were some Redemptorists in their nearby monastery. On the Sunday evening of the vision, four of the children had been sent to the Mother House in St Mary's to give a full account of the visitation. Beside themselves with excitement, they were passing Mount St Alphonsus when they spilled out their story to some Holy Fathers who were outside the church. Their story was received without doubt, the glorious tidings was related to the members of the Confraternity at their meeting the following evening.

The story then swept through the city causing no amount of excitement and speculation. The Bishop, Most Rev. Dr. G. Butler, made a statement prudently judging it best "to use caution in making it known" but he may as well have tried to stop the tide in the nearby Shannon such a firm hold had the story gained in the city. There were many enquires at the convent as to the verification of the story and these included, as the annals put it, "the proprietors of the two Liberal Papers" (unnamed).

On Monday night, following the announcement of the visions at the Confraternity meeting, members of that body approached the precincts of the convent and took their stand on the roads and fields in the vicinity of where the apparition took place. On Tuesday night, the numbers had increased considerably and Kenneally, the caretaker of the convent, got into trouble when allowing a few cronies into the grounds by means of a ladder. He reported that when passing the statue of Our Lady in front of the convent, a flash of light ascended and enveloped the statue with brilliant radiance. This was verified by some others, whom the caretaker found "gazing intently at the spot where in all its distinctness and grandeurs they beheld it too."

While the apparitions it seemed had been suspended, there was no diminution in the sensation, and each night ever increasing crowds assembled in the vicinity of the convent in the hope of seeing a reappearance of the visitation. The story had gained national and world wide attention and an excursion train from Cork brought a contingent of hopeful pilgrims.

Petitions flowed in. A. M. Conway, suffering from

distressing palsy, enclosed £10 to the Bishop for the Community and £1 for the orphans in Mount St Vincent's, begging their prayers which from recent events he hoped he might effectually obtain his relief. A lady in Glasgow asked them likewise for "the alleviation of domestic and pecuniary trails."

Still no sign of a repeat of the apparition, but it did not deter the crowds from turning up. As night succeeded night for more than a week following the apparition, the fields around the playground were literally crowded. Those who had no room therein stood in file, close as possible on the tops of the walls behind. Looking from the convent windows in the twilight "nothing less than a mass of human beings to an immense height" could be seen, for at this time enthusiasm had mounted to a degree that it could scarcely be possible to keep people from climbing over walls or giving them admittance by the gate." There the dense crowd stood or knelt till daybreak alternately reciting the Rosary and singing hymns.

At this stage, it was found necessary to close the grounds as the gardens began to be seriously damaged and its produce reduced to pulp by the vast crowds. And still they came, filling the roads in the vicinity and climbing on the walls.

An event now occurred which was the cause of much vexation to the Sisters and the Catholics of the city. In the vicinity of the convent lived a goodly number of those of a different persuasion to those who nightly sought to see the celestial vision. Their sleep disturbed nightly by the noise of the multitude and as the annals so grandiosely described it "demonstrations of religious beliefs and prayers uncongenial to their feelings, the resource of parties thus disaffected usually finds its outlet in representations of outrage perpetrated in the assemblies they wish to put a stop to."

What was described as one of the Liberal Journals got behind them and one of its writers, whom it was sadly claimed had been very sympathetic to the convent over the years, came out and wrote so derogatorily on the apparitions that it caused great pain to the community.

"We heard of one at least, Dr Doheny, Prior of the Augustinian Convent, who sent back the paper to the office whence it came to show his marked disapproval" it was noted by the annals.

Dr. Patrick Enright, taking up the cudgel on behalf of the nuns, entered the fray and wrote a letter to the offending newspaper full of frankness to restore "right to light." The letter was published and was followed by an apology of "regret and contradiction for assertions hastily made through misrepresentations."

Even though there was still no reappearance of the vision, interest was such that the *London Times* (described colourfully in the annals as "the great organ and advocate of England and the trumpeter of what can reflect on the dear Irish people") send an agent over to report on the apparitions and take photographs of the area where they took place.

The *Munster News*, published in Patrick Street, during the week carried two major articles on the apparition which tallied very much with what is recorded in the Mercy annals. It added that 7,000 were in the precincts of the convent on the Saturday after the apparitions were first seen and that there was widespread wonder at the statements made by a number of respectable citizens, to which they earnestly adhere, that on Friday night, they witnessed the apparition of the Blessed Virgin above the statue of Our Lady, and the wife of one of the number fainted, she was so overcome by the beauteous vision.

The report added: "Those who stated they saw the wonderful spectacles are unshaken in their belief that these appearances were due to no mortal influences, and there is no possible doubt on the subject. The scenes which have occurred almost every night have been unparalleled. More impressive manifestations of Catholic piety, and of unlimited faith in the intercession

Mount Vincent at the turn of the 19th century.

of the Mother of God, were never beheld in Ireland, and they could not be witnessed, even by the most sceptical and hardened, without emotion."

On the orphans who saw the vision, the report stated: "Several were from thirteen to fourteen years of age, and it was impossible not to be convinced of their truthfulness."

The last sighting by the orphans was on Tuesday the 17th and the following week, with no more major sightings reported, interest began to wane somewhat. The community in the Mount humbly accepted that they were not to join in the good fortune of the orphans in seeing the vision of Our Lady. "Twas not the will of the Almighty that any of the community, much as they longed for happiness, should get a distant glimpse of the celestial apparitions," the annals stated. However, there was some consolation on the Monday night in the sighting of what was described as wonderfully exquisite globes of light in the direction of the setting sun "as if they too should manifest a tribute to honour Heaven's Queen on her beloved visit to the land whose soil lies rich with the ashes of her most devoted servants, saints and martyrs, during centuries of cruel wrong and persecution."

Did the orphans genuinely see a vision of Our Lady or was it as some sceptics at the time said: "the result of lively imaginations, or images woven by electricity in the air after the thunderstorms?" Be that as it may, there were many who believed in the children's testimony, even some Protestants being convinced of the authenticity of the visions.

The annals wind up what was described as the Cherished Subject, without being able to give further evidence of the certainty of the heavenly Visions vouchsafed. "They shall like many similar ones remain shrouded in obscurity until the bright light of a better world take away all mystery, but we have carefully refrained from making statements except from those on whose judgment and veracity the community relied."

The annals colourfully wind up the affair thus: "How happy that the Holy Church leaves us unfettered and free in our simple convictions of those tokens of Divine Love and power granted to cheer and strengthen us in the rugged pathway of our exile here below, for while with unerring wisdom, she scrutinises cautiously and tests slowly things that are tangible out of natural order and watches over to preserve Her Children from illusion and deceit, her ways are not those of sceptics that require confirmation from our own eyes, but rather in her big-heartedness, benign and encouraging, to the soul seated longing of the Faithful generally, for glimpse of the Blissful Being from the unknown world to which their hopes and aspirations are ever fondly turned."

A few weeks previously, according to the Munster News, an apparition of the Blessed Virgin was reported to have been witnessed in the church in Newmarket-on-Fergus. On the feast day, the 15th, thousands from all over the country converged on the church, with two trains, each driven by two engines carrying thirty carriages, arriving from Limerick. So vast was the crowd, the newspaper reported, that thousands must have been able to see the edifice only from a distance. The previous year (1879) the Knock apparitions occurred.

Pictures of Yesteryear

Limerick Corporation pictured in 1951 during the tri-centenary celebrations commemorating the Siege of Limerick, 1651. Standing: F. Glasgow, M. O'Malley, J. J. Connery, J. Cuneen, G. B. Dillon, J. J. Finnan, P. J. Donnellan, C. Keyes, K. Bradshaw, S. Walsh. Front row; Ald. J.Reidy, T.D.; Ald. J. Carew, M. Macken, city manager; S. Coughlan, mayor; D. Bourke, T.D.; Ald. G. E.Russell. Absent: Councillors P. O'Connell and K. O'Sullivan.

Members of the Dominican Choir, circa 1960. Back row: M. McGuirk, J. Byrne, Miss Y. Costigan, J. Kenerk, Miss C. Doherty, J. Fitzgerald, T. Madden. Centre: Miss A. Byrne, C. Fitzgerald, Miss M. Killeen, Miss B. Keane, S. Ryan, Miss M. Mannion, Miss B. Cleary, D. Costigan, Miss M. Foley. Front: Miss R. Carey, Mrs. C. Clarke, Rev. F. Gerrard, O.P., Spiritual Director; Professor D. Guina, organist and choirmaster; P. Wallace, Mrs. T. Madden, Miss G. McGuirk

No less than 47 boys sang in the Redemptorist Choir in the early 1950's and are now well known citizens. The men in the back row are: N. Gantley, J. Quinn, P. Ring, T. Hannon, E. O'Sullivan (R.I.P.), D. Kelly (R.I.P.), R. Egleston (R.I.P.), S. Hannon, M. McNamara. 4th row: J. McGilligan, T. Liston, C. O'Mahony (R.I.P.), V. O'Connor, --, R. Murray, D. McNamara, G. Harran, E. Moloney, J. Harron, T. Kelly, --, --. 3rd row: --, R. O'Mahony, M. Roycroft, J. Fahey, D. Hilton, E. O'Connor, --, J. O'Mahony, F. Corr, N. Tuite, T. Drennan. 2nd row: B. Bradshaw, --, P. Roycroft, --, M. McMahon, N. Morgan, N. Harran, D. Hayes (R.I.P.), --, L. Neville, R. O'Donoghue, G. Lewis. Front: --, P. Sheahan, T. Roycroft --, V. Guerini, T. O'Donoghue, D. Cahill, A. Noonan, G. Gleeson, P. O'Brien, T. Moloney.

Coiste Cumann Gaelach Muire Fleadh na Nolag, pictured in St. Anne's Technical Institute in 1955. Back: Anne (Kennedy) Devereaux, Charlie Bartlett, Paddy Mulcahy, Dinny Max (well known ceili master), Tadhg O'Ceallaigh, N.T.; Breda Finucane. Front: Suzy Mulcahy, Fr. Wall, C.C, Effin; Kevin Bradshaw, former Mayor; Fr. Eamonn Casey, C.C., St. Patrick's; Chris O'Connell. At the very back is Annie Benson, renowned button accordion player, who played for the Cumann ceili's and other such Irish functions for many years, and Claire Carey.

A view of Pa Healy's Field taken from O'Dwyer Bridge in 1956. On the river are three angling cots, a larger version of the traditional Abbey Fishermen's brechauns. The cots were used extensively for angling, and for poling and rowing races in the Old Abbey, Plassey, and Corbally regattas. Below: The same view of Pa Healy's taken fifty years afterwards (2006), showing the Grove Island apartments

In 1968 the Pope reiterated the Church's teaching on the prohibition of contraception. Cartoonist Donellan captured the mood in the Leader of how Tom and Paschal took the news.

Limerick Golf Club, finalists in the Pierce Purcell Shield at Westport, 1990. Back: Joe McKenna, Ivan Morrissey, Brian Moroney, Billy O'Shea, Mick O'Donnell, Mick Aherne, Ger Malone, Bobby Roche, Seamus O'Sullivan. Front: Ted O'Donovan, Cyril Burkery, Ger Naughton, Austin Reid, club captain; Brendan Smyth, team captain; Stephen Carroll, Maurice Whelan.

The fields of Castletroy and other golfing stories

MANY moons ago, two Castletroy Golf Club members travelled to Lahinch for a game of golf. Before they departed for home that evening, they went into the clubhouse for a bite to eat and a drink or two. They noticed in the corner another member of their club slumped down and obviously the worse for wear from drink. They were not surprised, as this particular gentleman was well known for his excesses in this regard. The two golfers were charitable men, however, and being an August Monday night, they worried that

their fellow member would not be able to get home for work next day. They checked around to see if he had companions and finding none, dumped their wayward member into the back of their car and set course for home.

Arriving at his house in the suburbs of Limerick, they helped him to his front door but could not get an answer to their knocking. A neighbour eventually passed by and they asked if any of our friend's family were about.

'As far as I know the whole family is in Lahinch for the week!' was the reply.

It has not been recorded, but little imagination is needed, to guess the reaction of the various parties in this little drama to an act of charity that went famously wrong.

Another great story about Lahinch concerns the sixth hole (par three) famously known as the Dell, the green screened by a formidable dune which means a blind shot for the golfer. In the old days caddies, out of sight behind the dune, were not averse to tipping the odd ball belonging to Yanks into the hole to give the owner the great thrill of claiming a hole in one, and hopefully dispensing a large tip at the end of the round.

One day, back in the late 1940's, the formidable Bishop of Galway, Dr. Browne, was hitting off at the Dell from the tee-box just inside the wall skirting the Liscannor road. Some farming lads, a bit *maith go leor*, returning from a fair in Ennistymon, were passing at the time in their horse and cart and paused to see the Bishop, who was unknown to them (he was dressed in civies) tee off.

As luck would have it, the Bishop, possibly conscious of this unexpected rustic audience, miss-hit completely and sent the ball a few yards down the fairway. The boys in the cart fell around the place laughing, calling the now apoplectic bishop a right effin eejit.

The late Kevin Quin was the august secretary of Limerick G.C. for many years. A member of a great Limerick family identified with the early days of the motor car and radio in the city, he was an accomplished rugby player and referee, oarsman, tennis player and international boxing referee. He was an authority on the rules of the Royal and Ancient, and brusque to the point that those who did not know him thought him rude. The type if asked what colour tees you were playing off in competition, would reply 'that's what the notice board is for!'

Kevin, as was his wont, was looking out the window of his office one day when to his indignation he saw a male about to hit off the ladies' tee box, situated just beyond the men's. He rushed out and upbraided the miscreant, who with head bowed, took the flak.

'Are you finished?' he said to Kevin.

'Yes.'

'This is my third shot,' was the laconic reply.

A life-long friend, Joe O'Donovan, was playing Kevin for their usual half-crown one day, a bet which unfortunately Joe rarely managed to win. On the 7th hole (now the 14th) Joe was two up and feeling good when his ball nestled in an indention in front of the green.

'Can I take a drop?' Joe enquired.

'Certainly,' Kevin replied

Joe dropped the ball over his shoulder, as was the rule at he time, and duly halved the hole in par. He was about to hit off at the eighth when Kevin coughed and said 'my honour.'

'But we halved the last,' Joe replied indignantly.

'I won the hole,' Kevin claimed. 'If you had asked *may* I drop the ball instead of *can* I drop it I would have said yes, but under penalty.'

'It was a salutary lesson in the use of the English language and golf rules,' Joe recalled.

Another day three American visitors paid in dollars their green fees and Kevin, ever vigilant, watched as they teed off. Their attempts to drive off the first tee was so purile that it was obvious all three were beginners. Their round ceased there as Kevin, appalled at the thought of the abuse that lay in store for his beloved course, handed them back their green fees.

One of the great characters in Castletroy is Sean Meaney, still happily with us. A Korean War veteran, professional singer, entertainer and noted wit, he had a stint in the Danny Kaye film "The Five Pennies." A highly accomplished golfer, he played off a handicap of plus one in his prime.

Sean Meaney of Castletroy, who with a round of 63 broke the course record when winning the Scratch Cup at Athlone in 1969, receiving the cup from Mrs. M. de Lacy Staunton with Jack Spollen, captain, in centre.

Playing in a club fourball one day, Sean and his partner waited while one of a group of players hit off from a nearby tee-box. The player's tee shot was so bad his ball landed at Sean's feet.

"See that guy?" said Sean turning to his fellow players. "If he fell into a barrel of tits he'd come out sucking his thumb."

Sean's opponents laughed so much they lost the vital hole to the entertainer and his partner Pat Cross.

Jimmy Clinch of Baltray was playing in the Castletroy Golf Club Scratch Cup one time and had approached the 11th tee, a hole which has a sharp dog leg to the right, with the green guarded by tall trees. Worried that if he did not draw his ball accurately he might wind up on the road, he asked caddy Alfie Bennett if the hole was driveable over the trees.

"Sean Meaney used do it regularly," replied Alf.

"Well, if that son of a gun could do it, so can I," replied Clinch.

Clinch, reputed to be one of the longest hitters in Europe, took a mighty drive, his ball soaring over the trees and heading for the green. Sadly, it dipped at the last minute and clattered into the branches.

"I thought you said Meaney used drive this regularly," Clinch said to the caddy through clenched teeth."

"He did indeed sir, but there was no trees there that time!"

In a more relaxed era when japes were not uncommon, Sean and his golfing cohorts used get up to all sorts of devilment. Relaxing afterwards in the bar after a game in Ballybunion one day he bet his fellow Limerickmen he'd go round the holes running parallel to the road (which included back to back par fives) in five shots.

His compatriots quite rightly scoffed at the idea, and those who thought there was handy money to be made, put up tidy sums on the counter.

They all trooped out to the first tee to see Sean attempting the impossible.

Sean excused himself and re-appeared in his car and parked alongside the first tee. He opened the booth, chipped his ball in, and with several hanging on the car, set off down the course to complete the wager. When he arrived at the last of the designated holes, he got into the booth, chipped the ball onto the green, and got down in three to record his five.

A veteran Limerick G.C. member, who had reached the eighty mark, was asked some years back if he had his entry in for the father and son competition, which had just been initiated in the club.

"You must be joking me," was the terse reply. "Sure my dad is dead for the past thirty years!"

Shannon Golf Club in its early days had as a member a very keen but volatile golfer. One day some of the members were in the bar when word came through that our friend (whom we shall name Tommy) was after dumping his bag into the lake in the middle of what was obviously a horrendous round.

They watched as Tommy came storming towards the clubhouse.

"Ah, he'll go back for it you'll see," said one of the members.

"I don't think so," replied another.

They had a bet on the outcome.

Tommy reached the precincts of the clubhouse. They watched as he hesitated and then making up his mind, he stormed back out on the course.

The member who bet Tommy would retrieve the bag was elated.

They waited. Tommy came back again, without the bag.

"Are you alright there Tommy," one of the members shouted down.

"I am but the bag isn't. I shagged it into the lake but went back to get my car keys out of it."

One day in Kilkee, a beginner was setting out on his round. He made a few unsuccessful attempts to hit the ball, his partner urging him to keep his head down. When he eventually connected, his ball landed on the road, narrowly missed a cyclist who feel off his bike, and a motorist nearly drove over the cliff attempting to avoid him.

"Oh my God, what do I do now?" cried the beginner.

'Maybe if you adjusted your grip a bit," replied his helpless partner.

Putting is one of the most frustrating parts of a golfer's game. On a good day the hole seems as a big as a bucket, on bad, as small as an egg-cup. Back in the 1930's an eccentric American professional was playing in a tournament in which he had a horrendous final round thanks to a putter that would do anything but put the ball in the hole. Before setting out for home he got some string and hung the errant putter off the rear bumper of his car. When asked what he was up to he replied: "That son-of-a bitch made me suffer today and by God it's gonna suffer now."

Argentinean golfer Rodriguez, asked one time about his putting, stated: "I never pray to God to make a putt, but I pray to God to help me react good if I miss one."

Unlike mundane Sky golf commentators, Americans commentators can be witty. During one broadcast from the States, a player's ball went into the hole but popped out again. "I guess that ball is just afraid of the darkness," was the witty observation of the commentator.

David Feherty, one of the wittiest broadcasters on the American scene, during his playing days was confronted with a snake on the tee-box when playing in South Africa. Asked to comment on a round that was not very distinguished, he said it was anaconda the fright he got from the snake.

Golf has many quaint sayings. 'You're on the dance floor' is an expression used when someone lands their ball on the green. A Salaman Rushdi green is one that is hard to read. Your opponent is your friend when his shot lands in the bunker but a bastard when it lands in the middle of the green.

Dermot Gilleece, the eminent golf correspondent in the *Sunday Independent*, has recalled a story by Mark McCormack, the legendary golf promoter, the essence of which is English snobbery.

All his life, a distinguished English barrister wanted to play Sandringham G.C. And though aware of its status as a very exclusive club, he one day picked up the courage to approach the secretary.

'Member?' he was asked. 'No sir.' 'Guest of a member?' 'No sir.' 'Sorry.'

As he turned to leave, the lawyer happened to see a familiar figure seated in the lounge reading *The Times*. It was Lord Wellesley of Park. So he approached him and said: 'I beg your pardon your lordship but my name is Higginbottom from the London law firm of Higginbottom, Willoughby and Barclay and I'd like to ask you a huge favour. I wish to play this delightful course as your guest.'

His lordship gave Higginbottom a rather long look before enquiring 'Church?' 'Episcopalian sir, the late wife, Church of England.' 'Education?' 'Eton and Oxford.' 'Sports?' 'Rugby, sir, a spot of tennis and I rowed No. 4 in the crew that beat Cambridge.' 'What about military?' 'Coldstream Guards, VC and Knight of the Garter.' 'Campaign?' 'Dunkirk, El Alamein, Normandy.' 'Languages?' 'Private Tutor in French, fluent German and a bit of Greek.' His lordship thought for a minute and then turned to the club secretary and said: 'Nine holes.'

A golfing fanatic was playing with his wife one day when after an errant drive his ball landed in front of the green-keepers' shed. Furious at the thought of dropping a shot or two, his wife suggested that she open the two sliding doors which would give him a shot to the green. He complied, but sadly, just as he hit, his wife stuck her head round the door. The ball got her in the middle of her forehead, and she expired on the spot.

Some years later he was playing in the club fourball when he found his ball exactly in the same spot. His partner suggested that he slide open the two doors to afford him a shot to the green but the widower was horrified at the suggestion.

'I can't. I tried that some years ago and something awful happened.'

'What was that?' enquired the partner.

'I took a seven.'

A hacker nearing the end of another inglorious round turned to his caddie and said 'I'd move heaven and earth to break a hundred on this course.'

Caddie: Try heaven, you've already moved most of the earth.'

Golfer: 'You must be the worst caddie in the world.'

Caddie: 'That'd be too much of a coincidence.'

A well known local enthusiast was telling a non-golfing workmate about a super round of golf he had the previous day. 'And I wouldn't mind,' he added, 'but I hadn't played for months. I sometimes find the less I play the better the round of golf on my return.

'What you should do now,' replied the workmate, 'is give it up completely and you'd be brilliant altogether!'

Finally, *I wish I hadn't said that*: Jack Nicklaus back in 1994, when asked about the failure of coloured golfers to make a significant breakthrough in the P.G.A. Tour, is purported to have said: 'that black athletes didn't have the right muscles for golf.'

In the era of parcels from America, these youngsters from Mill View Terrace in the Sandmall, were enjoying the delights of the Shannon in their family huts in Corbally in the late 1940's. Back: Marie Flannery, Joan and Noreen O'Shaughnessy. Front: Rita Flannery, Betty McBride and Kay Flannery. In the background is St. Thomas' Island and Crowe's house in Parteen, since demolished. *(Quinn Collection)*

Parcel from America

ONE would have to be of a certain generation to appreciate what a parcel from America meant to an Irish household of the 1940's or 1950's. In an era of huge scarcity, the arrival of the big, brown paper wrapped parcel, with the invariable image of George Washington on the stamps, was akin to Christmas dawning unannounced.

What treasures did it contain? There would surely be frocks for the womenfolk. Frocks with gay patterns that would laugh at the sombre colours of a depressed war and post-war era. Scented soap to replace the grim Lifebouy and Carbolic (if one were lucky to get it). A sports coat for dad maybe with shoulder pads so wide you'd think the hanger was left in them. Certainly neck ties, as wide as scarves, and Hawaiian grass-skirted native girls painted on them and they dancing and waving their hands under the palm trees.

Excitement was unconfined as mam, usually flushed

to the gills, fumbled with the string and brown paper to uncover the cardboard box that would surely contain undreamed of bounty. Expectancy was unbearable as each layer unfolded, to reveal the Aladdin cave of treasure that expectant eyes were sure it contained.

If we were at school we missed this, the best part. Our benefactor was our Aunt Ciss in New York but sadly for the males in the family, it was the household's six women folk who normally scored. She was a seamstress in a New York hospital and all of the clothes she sent were of the female gender. Two nurses' walking out uniforms were included one year, consisting of smart suits, pill-box hats, and shoulder bags, and sisters Maura and Eileen were the talk of the parish as they paraded in the outfits to admiring glances from neighbours in the Sandmall and Athlunkard Street.

An enormous parcel arrived one day and we could hardly wait for the many layers of brown paper to be uncovered. Here be treasures we thought, the delicious anticipation of what the package contained being possibly the highlight of the whole parcel ethos. Alas, most of the package was taken up with this enormous teddy bear type of fur coat you would have seen in films such as *The Great Gatsby*. You would imagine that such a treasure would be to die for, but such was the bulk and vintage of Auntie Ciss' offering that the females cast a snoot and the coat was cast ingloriously into the press to become a plaything for the younger members of the family.

That was until one freezing night when my sister Eileen was attending a dress dance. "You'll be needing a fur coat tonight 'tis so cold," announced my mother as she rescued the coat and dusted it down. "I'll be grand mam, I have my own coat," cried Eileen in desperation. But to no avail. The teddy bear coat it had to be and we watched her diminutive figure depart into the night, her face barely discernable in the mountain of fur. Embarrassed she was, but she sure was cosy.

And then there was the confirmation outfit. Imagine the reaction of a sophisticated young girl of today being told that she would be making her Confirmation in a dress fashioned from a bath robe! Such was the fate of my sister Joan. She took the sacrament in such a garment, which had its origins in the robe from Auntie Ciss' parcel. She wasn't too happy about it, but then it was an era of huge deprivation, the Second World War just having ended. She often slagged mam in later years, "the only child in St Mary's to have made her Confirmation in a bath robe."

Brother Joe and myself did have small consolation prizes such as pencils with erasers attached to the end, an innovation that caused great wonder and exclamations of "what will they think of next?" We were the envy of schoolmates, and we went back to being mere mortals when the erasers eventually wore out.

Auntie also included the inevitable sticks of Wrigley's chewing gum which we chewed for hours on end, and we held our breaths to see if she included some *Dell* comics. With just the *Dandy* and the *Beano* to entertain us up to this, a whole new world was opened up to us with *The Lone Ranger* crying *Hi Silver*; *Superman*, and *Batman* soaring through the skyscrapers of New York in pursuit of deadly villains. When finished with them, we could swap these pristine comics for several well worn one from the likes of cute broker Walter Stanley from River Lane in the Abbey.

As we have stated, rarely was there clothes for the males included in Auntie Ciss' parcels, but looking at some of the loud and gaudy attires of neighbouring boyhood recipients, and the accompanying jeering comments, maybe we felt we weren't too deprived after all.

Another aunt, this time the unique and formidable Nancy Lynch from Athlunkard Street, in her US sojourn, was fairy godmother to the Browner family in Dublin. Dad was Connie, noted rugby player and singer, and formerly from O'Dwyer Villas. Listen to daughter Frances, delightfully and vividly describe youthful wonder at the treasures unearthed in the parcel from America.

'You always knew when an American parcel had arrived. You could tell the minute you walked in the back door from school. There was an air of excitement about the place, the kitchen in disarray with papers and strings and colourful boxes and unfamiliar odds and ends scattered all over. And you would know by my mother's face. Her black curls flopped untidily into her forehead, a smile beamed from her lips, and she chatted non-stop, an octave higher than we were used to.

'There was a certain smell, too, of what I could not tell you, but it surely was a welcome change from the soap powder and baking aromas to which we were accustomed.

'My heart would skip a beat at the sight of the two large cardboard boxes, standing three feet high, in the middle of the room. There would be clothes everywhere: spilling out of the boxes, draped across the chairs, flung on the floor. And there were always matching outfits for me and my two sisters.

'I can remember a green velvet pinafore with pearl buttons and a lace collar. A red corduroy one too, that had a white blouse underneath, which we wore in the family snapshot at Christmas.

'Daffodil cotton dresses and straw hats with yellow ribbons announced the arrival of springtime. We wore them to Mass on Easter Sunday and even clutched American prayer books in our pudgy little hands. I was as proud as if I had been walking down Fifth Avenue in the Easter Parade.

'Floral anoraks brightened up summer showers and navy duffel coats carried us through many's the tough Irish winter,

'Once I got a pink watch with a pink strap, the likes of which I loved to show off when raising my hand in Mrs. Griffin's fourth class in the primary school. 'Pandora would have been envious of such treasures – rows and rows of chewing gum which fell into our laps like an open accordion, gooey sweets and chocolates that stuck to our teeth and locked our jaws in delirium. Betty Crocker cake mixes in mysterious hues of blue and green, far more preferable that Ma's homemade scones and tarts.

'Best of all were the sugared ice cream cones – but alas! No ice cream! The flavours suggested on the box, however, were enough to make us yearn to fly off to the golden land which offered such delight'.

A delightful and extraordinary detailed recall you will agree, an account which was published in the *East Hampton Star*. The extended family of Aunt Nan, as Nancy Lynch was fondly called, threw a memorable hooley in the Shannon RFC Pavilion to honour her on her ninetieth birthday in 1994, and she lived on for several more years. Who knows, but she may be still sending parcels to the Browners, this time from heaven, and in another form.

Did you know that there's even been a musical written about the Parcel from America for God's sake? Tomaseen Foley is the composer, and the musical is set in Teampall an Ghleantainn. It depicts the sadness of an elderly widow, watching out for the arrival of a Christmas parcel from her only errant son (the only eye in the spud) that never arrives, and how the neighbours rally around to create for her an unforgettable Christmas.

Interestingly, Ireland was not unique regarding parcels from America. During the height of World War II, literally thousands of parcels arrived weekly from the States to families in England, donated by sympathetic Yankee families, aware of the deprivations being suffered by the besieged populace. By June, 1942 the volume of parcels had grown to such an extent that prime minister Winston Churchill was obliged to write to US President Roosevelt requesting a serious diminution of the flow. He wrote:

'The generosity of your people has been overwhelming and the parcels from America have become a familiar and welcome feature in all the misfortunes that have overtaken our civilian population. However, due to additional demands being made on shipping resulting from the enormously increased flow of war materials for which ocean transport has to be provided, I request regretfully, that the flow of these parcels should now be greatly diminished. We shall therefore have to assign to goods of a more warlike character the shipping space which has hitherto been available for the relief of our people - a sacrifice which we will make here without complaint, but not without very great regret. I cannot conclude this letter, Mr. President, without affirming once again our gratitude for the comfort in the days of suffering and of trial that were brought about by the people of America, and our desire to make known our thanks. *Winston S. Churchill.'*

Mr. Roosevelt replied:

'I am gratified by your statement that the relief sent from this country has given comfort to the British people during their days of great trial, and I shall give to the American people your expression of appreciation for the gifts they have provided. I am convinced that their action is indicative of the profound admiration felt in this country for the heroic stand of the British people against a barbarous foe.

'You may be assured that we shall co-operate in every feasible way with the American Gifts Committee in order to meet the situation brought about by the increased demand for shipping. *Franklin D. Roosevelt.'*

Many women from St. Mary's acted as extras in John Ford's Rising of the Moon filmed in the vicinity of King John's Castle in 1956. They were paid ten shillings a day but those being paid dole money were docked accordingly.

St. John's Newfoundland, at the time of the shipwreck of the Francis Spaight.

Full story of the *Francis Spaight*

ON 18th December, 1835, Timothy Gorman, the skipper of the Limerick registered sailing barque, the *Francis Spaight*, gave his crew an incredible choice. His ship had been wrecked by a fierce snowstorm on December 5th, nine days out from St John's in New Brunswick, with three crew members being washed overboard. Only for its cargo of timber, the vessel would have foundered, but was now immersed with water to the deck, all sails having being lost. All provisions and drinking water were fouled and the fifteen man crew, without any sustenance for over two weeks (except for two bottles of wine between them) faced imminent starvation.

The captain, calling his crew together on the icy, water-filled deck, gave them a stark choice. Either agree that one of the crew be killed and cannibalised so that the others might survive, or face certain starvation. He assured them that traditions of the sea allowed such a drastic course of action, and that there would be no recriminations. There would be a fair casting of lots.

How different it had all started out eight months earlier when the smart, three masted barque was launched and registered in Limerick by its proud owner, timber importer Francis Spaight. In the mode of the time, it was named after its owner. Spaight, magistrate, landlord, and leading merchant in the south, assisted many of his tenants to emigrate to Canada from his estate in Derry Castle, above Ballina, North Tipperary, adjacent to Lough Derg.

The landlord had described the estate "as the most over populated in Britain" and he had purchased it in

1843 "in a state of wrack and ruin." He gave valuable information on famine conditions and emigration to a select committee of the House of Commons in "Black '47," the year most associated with the catastrophic failure of the potato crop in Ireland.

The *Francis Spaight*, three-masted, burthen 370 tons and 108 feet in length, had a dual purpose, being used for transporting emigrants, mostly to North America, and on its return journey bringing back cargoes of timber. On one of its first voyages, Gorman had been censured for not providing enough provisions for the passengers, many embarking in a haggard condition in St. John's. Spaight, however, had the reputation of being one of the more enlightened and humane landlords and insisted that his ships took a whole family or none when emigrating.

Two hundred and sixteen passengers were transported by the *Francis Spaight* to New Brunswick in the month of May, 1835, with Kilrush born Gorman again as captain. For some unknown reason, the ship was delayed in St. John's and it was November 24 before she left on her ill-fated voyage to Limerick with a cargo of timber.

Nothing was heard from the ship until early January when an urgent letter was sent to Spaight from the Master of the Port of Falmouth, England. Its melancholy contents were published in the *Limerick Chronicle* of January 13, 1836, to the grief and consternation of the families of the crew and the citizens of Limerick in general.

The barque, according to the newspaper account, ran into a fierce snowstorm on the night of December 3rd, nine days out from St. John's. The ship was struck by heavy seas while lying to, which threw her on her beam-ends and it quickly became partially submerged. Huge waves now swept over the stricken craft and three of the crew, the mate William Griffiths, and two hands, Pat Cusack and Pat Behane, were swept overboard and drowned.

By great exertion, the crew cut away the weather lanyards of the fore and main rigging, which leaving the masts unsupported, they soon went overboard, and she righted. The ship barely floated due to its cargo of timber. The remainder of the nineteen strong crew now faced starvation as all provisions were washed away and the fresh water fouled. Their sole sustenance was a few bottles of port wine and what rainwater they could collect by whatever means available.

With the ship now completely waterlogged, and seas running over its deck, the crew had to stand permanently in water, holding on to whatever immovable object they could find. The cabin under the poop was also awash but it at least it provided some bit of shelter from the biting wind. Here the wretched survivors gathered, holding on by whatever means possible, and they leant against one another for support.

After several days in this desperate situation, sores began to break out on the legs of the crew due to the constant immersion in salt water. These proved extremely painful, especially if they hit against some object. The sails of two ships were sighted in the following days but they were too far away to spot the stricken vessel.

After about two weeks of this extreme deprivation (accounts of exactly how long vary) several of the men started to show signs of deep distress. With no sign of rescue in sight, Captain Gorman called the stricken crew together He stated that it was now impossible to sustain themselves any longer without food and water and suggested the only course open to them was that one should die so that the remainder should survive on the corpse. He also suggested that lots should be cast amongst the ship's four apprentice boys as their loss would not be as great as that of the crew, all of whom were married and had families.

The crew unanimously decided on this course of action, the only objection coming from 15-year-old apprentice Patrick O'Brien, who lived with his widowed mother in Thomondgate, on the outskirts of Limerick City. Accounts say that he agreed there was need to cast lots but that all of the crew should be included.

As luck would have it, on a date between the 18th and the 22nd December, it was O'Brien himself who drew the shortest straw. He was tied up and his eyes bandaged as the unwilling ship's cook, captain's namesake John Gorman, on the orders of the captain, went about his grisly business of cutting the wrists of the unfortunate apprentice.

The crew watched in horror as the cook took the boy's wrists and made incisions with a pen knife.

Unfortunately the blood did not flow freely and the boy, now highly agitated, made to cut the wrists himself. He was also unsuccessful and the captain ordered the cook to cut the apprentice's throat, a suggestion which O'Brien resisted strongly, screaming that anyone who touched him, he would come back to haunt them. He was held down and the cook completed the grisly job.

The crew fed on the corpse for a few days, but several of them now began to show sings of insanity, some having drank sea water. The cook was amongst the worst affected, and a few days later, as he showed signs of expiring, it was decided that he would be the next to die. He was executed and the several of the crew were reported to have drank his blood. Another apprentice, George Byrnes, now showed signs of expiring and he too met the fate of the cook and his fellow apprentice. Crew member Michael Behane was also about to be killed, but he saved his executioner the bother by dying beforehand.

It was only the most hardened of the ill-fated crew that were now able to withstand the sight of the terrible carnage and their grim survival on the remains of their fellow crew members. Even the strongest now began to show signs of capitulation to madness and it was like a miracle when two days before Christmas, on the morning of December 23rd, the stricken vessel was spotted by the American registered brig, *Agenora*, which

affected a rescue of the crew at great peril to the lives of the captain, John Jellard, and the crew of the long boat. Rescues of stricken ships was a dangerous thing in the days of sailing craft as sails had to be trimmed and the rescue boat launched and manned amidst great danger. It was not unknown for captains to sail away from wrecks and leave stricken crews to their fate if conditions were too dangerous.

However, the ten surviving crew members, and the captain of the *Francis Spaight* were safely brought aboard the *Angenora* and were landed in the port of Falmouth. They were in a desperate state. Twenty excruciating days had passed since the storm of December 3rd. The letter from the Master of Falmouth described their condition "as being so miserable that it is difficult to describe."

The crew were housed in the workhouse in

Below deck in an emigrant ship. Francis Spaight, one of the most prominent merchants in the South of Ireland, had the reputation of being one of the more humane ship and landowners, and insisted that when families emigrated from his holdings in Castle Derry, Lough Derg, they would go as a complete uni

Falmouth, where they were fed and given clothes. When they made a recovery of sorts, a collection was got up to bring them home. In late January, 1836, the arrival of the survivors back in Limerick caused intense excitement, and according to the late Jim Kemmy, in a brief account of the tragedy in his *Limerick Anthology*, the captain and crew were tried for murder and acquitted. However, Brian Simpson, in his book, *Cannibalism and the Common Law*, contradicts this, writing that despite Francis Spaight being himself a justice of the peace, no legal proceedings against captain or crew were even contemplated.

An appeal was straight away made by Spaight for the alleviation of distress of the wretched crew and was published in the *Chronicle* on January 23. In the appeal, printed on opposite page, he declined to go into detail on the harrowing fate of those who died it was so shocking, claiming they were all drowned.

In appealing to the public on behalf of the eleven survivors of the crew of this ill-fated ship, and on behalf of the families of the seven who were drowned, or who perished under still more horrifying circumstances, it is not designed to enter into those details which, at the same time that they would awake the sympathies, would shock the feelings of the benevolent.

It is only necessary to state here that the surviving sufferers have arrived in Limerick in a state of abject wretchedness, and some of them are mutilated by the frost and otherwise rendered helpless, so as to be unable not only to obtain present bread, but to labour for it during the rest of their lives. Without food, without clothing (save the few articles given them by the inhabitants of Falmouth, where they had landed, to enable them to pass to this town), and without hope, unless from the present appeal, they and the families of their deceased shipmates, implore the bounty of the citizens, praying of them to recollect, that their destitution arises out of a Divine visitation, and that they bow under afflictions not produced by themselves. Subscriptions will be thankfully received by Francis Spaight, esq.

One would imagine that after this heartfelt and poignant appeal, that Spaight himself would have headed the subscription list. This was not so, the infamous Clare landlord, Crofton M. Vandeleur, donating £20 compared to Spaight's £10. Average subscriptions were £1, coming from prominent citizens and merchants, including the Mayor; Thomas Gabbett: James Bannatyne, John Norris Russell, Pierce Shannon, Mullock & Sons. In all, around £70 was collected.

When the full story of the grisly happenings on the *Francis Spaight* came out, it was not surprising that family members of those who were cannibalised took great exception.

Stories survive in Limerick of the harassment of the crew that followed, and the demented state the widow O'Brien got into on hearing of the circumstances of the death of her son Patrick. She claimed her son had died because the lots had been rigged.

She began a campaign of harassment and stalking against Captain Gorman who had to take out a court order binding her to the peace. He claimed in court that since he had returned from the voyage he had received no peace on account of the defendant who threatened to take away his life and that of his children as well. The widow claimed that all she did was to go on her knees in front of him begging him for details of her son's death, and instead of that he abused her.

One of the stories of the widow's harassment of Gorman has been related by Frank Prendergast, former Mayor of Limerick and esteemed historian He has recounted how down through the generations in his family the story of a forebear witnessing the captain being hassled by the widow as he made his way to Mass has been handed on. Falling on her knees and opening out her hair with her hands (an old custom of keening or mourning) she cursed and harangued the misfortunate man.

Another great mariner, Captain Kevin Donnelly, long associated with the Limerick Harbour Commissioners, has recounted that an old Limerick seaman told him that he was once asked by a shipmate in Liverpool, "are you one of the crew that ate the galley boy?"

Spaight himself did not escape the widow's ire either. She travelled out to his country house on one occasion, and witnesses said "her hysterical cries were truly heart-rendering," according to Simpson. Other crew members were also harassed by the families of those cannibalised in their homes along the shores of the Shannon.

But it was the captain who received most of the flak and according to local maritime historian James McMahon he erected a lamp over the door of his house at No. 77 O'Connell Street so that those knocking at his door after dark could be identified. He was seemingly a strong man, well able to defend himself, and received many more commissions from Spaight and other ship-

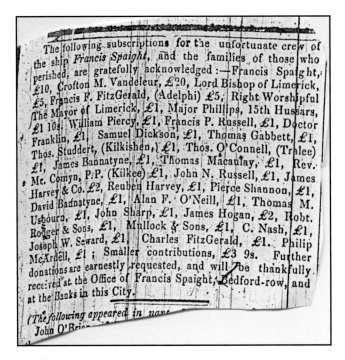

owners. He eventually moved to Dublin where he died in 1874, and is buried in an unmarked grave.

Gorman's brother, Daniel, also a skipper employed by Spaight, was nicknamed the lucky captain locally due to the fact that he was alleged never to have lost a ship. He is reputed to have transported up to 10,000 emigrants safely across the Atlantic. He is buried in St Munchin's Graveyard, opposite King John's Castle. Interestingly, the late historian Kevin Hannan has recorded that one of the crew members who survived was the ship's carpenter, Thomas Crehan, who later moved with his family to America. His daughter Ada, taking the stage name of Rehan, was to become one of that country's most celebrated Shakespearean actors. In later years a Liberty Ship was named after her.

The Francis Spaight was eventually salvaged and returned to service. It foundered off the coast of South Africa afterwards with the loss of four lives. It was the same amount, ironically, of the crew that was cannibalised so to that their fellow crew members should live.

The writer, Jack London, wrote a short, semi-fictional account of the tragedy (*The Francis Spaight: A True Story Retold*) but the tale he wove was not worthy of such a celebrated writer. He showed the crew up in the worst possible light, resorting to stage-Irish utterings of the stricken men, in the mode of the satirical *Punch* magazine which at the time caricatured the Irish as sub-human.

Not surprisingly, many myths have spring up over the years about the *Francis Spaight*. A particularly gruesome one is that the crew waved the hands and feet of the slaughtered apprentice O'Brien from the deck of their ship to draw attention to their plight, so terrified were they that the *Agenora* would not stop to rescue them. Another was that the captain was in the act of eating the liver and brains of his apprentice when the *Agenora* hove to.

The ship's owner is still remembered as his company, *Francis Spaight and Sons*, are still registered as timber importers, one hundred and seventy one years after the *Francis Spaight* was involved in the most celebrated case of cannibalism at sea.

Ballads were very popular at the time, and it is not surprising, given the magnitude of the event, that several were written about the *Francis Spaight*. One very accurate account (*The Sorrowful Fate of O'Brien*) has been preserved in James N. Healy's Irish Ballads and Songs of the Sea. This excerpt from the ballad describes the apprentices' fate thus

While lots they were preparing, those poor unfortunate boys
Stood gazing at each other with salt tears in their eyes.
A bandage o'er O'Brien's eyes they quickly did tie
For the second lot that was pulled up said O'Brien was

to die.

He said unto his comrade boys, 'Now let my mother
  know
The cruel death I did sustain, when you to Limerick go.'
Then John O'Gorman he was called to bleed him in the
  vein
Twice he tried to take his blood, but it was all in vain.

Our captain cried, 'Cheer up my boys, this work will
  never do;

O'Gorman you must cut his throat, or else you will die
  too.'
The trembling cook, he took the knife, which sore did
  him confound,
He cut his throat and drank his blood, as it flowed from
  the wound.

Early the next morning, the weather it got clear,
And the American Agenora, in sight she did appear.
Providence sent her that way for to protect our lives.
We're safe once more on Limerick's shore with our
  children and our wives.

The Custom House painted by W.H. Bartlett at the time of the story of the Francis Spaight.

Limerick's Grand Prix in Pictures

Limerick held centre-stage in the motor racing world when in 1935 and 1936 the Grand Prix was held through the city streets. Most of the top drivers from Europe took part and the race attracted wide attention. It was an era when motor racing was highly popular with titled people and one of the contestants was the Prince of Siam, Prince Birabongse, who attracted much attention. Photo shows the grand stand and spectators gathering before the race outside Todds.

Photograph shows the crude pedestrian bridge erected at the junction of Cecil Street during the Grand Prix. with two women cyclists chatting nonchalantly out on the road. The Royal George Hotel is to the right. Titled Englishman John Fitzroy, 9th Duke of Grafton, was tragically killed in 1936 when his car went out of control as it left the narrow bend at Roxboro. It was said the tragedy was one of the reasons the Grand Prix fell through after that.

AT A MEETING

OF THE

Magistrates, Visitors & Lodge-Owners of Kilkee,

Held on the 7th of August 1833,

LORD MASSY BEING CALLED TO THE CHAIR

The following Resolutions were adopted:

RESOLVED,

That we have witnessed the disgraceful practice of Bathing on the Strand of Kilkee, at all hours of the day, to the great annoyance of Females, who are, by such indecent exposures, prevented from exercising on the Beach.

That it is expedient that some measures be adopted to prevent a recurrence of the practice; and with this view, it is Resolved, that the Strand shall be divided into three parts; that two sides thereof, to the right and left, shall be appropriated to the use of the Female Visitors, for Bathing and that the portion of the Strand , defined by Posts in the centre, shall be for the use of the Male part of the Visitors, up to the Hour of Ten O' Clock in the Morning of each Day, but after that Hour, no Male Person shall be permitted to Bathe on the Strand.

That we are determined, by every means in our power, to put an end to the shameful custom which prevails, of naked men riding horses through the water; and that the Police shall receive instructions to seize all persons so offending, in order that they may be prosecuted according to Law; and that all Male Persons, bathing on the Strand after the prescribed hour, shall be also prosecuted.

MASSY.

Lord Massy having left the chair, and the Hon, Mr. Butler being called thereto,

RESOLVED,

That the thanks of this Meeting are due, and herby given, to Lord Massy, for his Lordship's dignified and very proper deportment in the Chair.

T.F.W. BUTLER, Chairman.

Printed at Canters Paper and Account-book Ware-house, 12, Francis Street, Limerick

Nude bathing in Kilkee: a prickly subject

Those were the days! Cheeky males disporting themselves in Myles' Creek near the Pollock Holes in Kilkee, in early 20th century. In Georgian and early Victorian times, males swam naked on the beach (see leaflet dating from 1833 on left) until they were eventually banished to Byrnes' Cove and the Pollock Holes (R. Coughlan collection)

IN late Georgian times, it was the accepted norm that in Kilkee, men bathed unrestrainedly in the nude. The beach was the favoured place for baring all, and even when horse-riding on the strand, they cheekily rode along the seashore in the buff. This carry-on caused huge inconvenience and great resentment amongst the ladies who unlike the feminists of today, meekly accepted that for all intents and purposes that the beach was out of bounds to them while the cheeky males bared all as they disported themselves and their horses in the

A view of Kilkee in Victorian times showing in the centre, bathing boxes, which were required to be used by swimmers for changing as there was a bye-law in place which forbade undressing on the beach.

briny. This was an era when Charlotte Bronte (author of *Jayne Ayre*) on honeymoon in Kilkee and staying in the West End Hotel, had to ask permission from her husband to sit alone for a little while on the cliffs contemplating the ocean!

Things were about to change for the better for the enraged women, however, when a shining knight appeared on the horizon, in the form of Lord Massey of Castleconnell, who in 1833 chaired a special meeting of magistrates, visitors and lodge owners in Kilkee "to take steps to counteract what was described as a shameful custom of naked men bathing and riding horses through the water, and that the police shall receive instructions to seize all persons so offending" (see leaflet).

The naked bathers were eventually banished from the beach and driven out to Byrnes' Cove, Myles' Creek and the Pollock Holes where they bottomed out. There, in their bare all, they reigned supreme for well over a century until the modern day feminists caught up with them with their pants down. There are now just a handful of the traditionalists still trying to hold on to what they call their traditional rights.

In an era of great moral rectitude in Victorian times, there were several bye-laws put in place by Kilkee Town Commissioners regarding bathing on the beach. For instance, if you wanted to go for a swim with your wife you risked prosecution: no mixed bathing was allowed. And if a man or woman modestly divested themselves of their clothes and donned their bathing togs on the strand, they too, were breaking the law: no undressing on the beach was allowed.

This is where bathing boxes came in and all old photographs of the strand show the quaint wooden boxes complete with wheels lined up near the water mark waiting to receive the chaste swimmers. So the bathing box it had to be if you wanted a swim. How they coped for the crowd on a hot August bank holiday, is not recorded.

With all these regulations in place it sure was a tough time for bathers, and one wonders how they bothered at all. Let "Neptune", writing to the Editor of the *Limerick Leader* in August 1919, reveal the frustrations of our forebears planning a dip in the briny in the Queen of the West:

"Dear Sir – Reading a letter in a recent issue of your paper prompted me to write on another aspect prevailing at Kilkee, namely mixed bathing and undressing on the strand. The visitor to Kilkee is told that mixed bathing will not be allowed on the strand. Can the Improvement Committee tell anyone where the female relatives can be taught to swim, except on the strand? I am going there every year and cannot find a place to teach swimming. I know several male friends who cannot get their wives to go out on the strand principally on account of this foolish restriction.

"Another ridiculous bye-law is about the prohibition of undressing on the strand. Surely there would be no reason for this if the Committee provided sufficient bathing boxes. It is nothing unusual to hear of ladies waiting two hours for the use of one, and if every person was to use the battered wrecks* there at present we

Forbidden fruit: This couple faced prosecution as mixed bathing was taboo in Victorian Kilkee.

should have plenty of moonlight bathing. Anyone undressing on the stand is not doing it from lack of modesty, but solely to get finished bathing as soon as possible.

"I have no wish to discredit Kilkee – in fact I would not enjoy a holiday elsewhere – but that now there is such keen competition for visitors everywhere the Committee should be alive and strong and provide a portion of the strand where a man can teach a lady to swim.

"Every year we hear of people going to the Isle of Man, Tramore, Youghal, and other seaside resorts and coming back with glowing accounts of how visitors are catered for. You never hear the same of Kilkee. Surely there must be something wrong. Thanking you for insertion.– NEPTUNE."

The previous year (1918) eleven bathing boxes on the strand, belonging to Messrs. J. and T. Brann, were wrecked in a fierce storm which occurred on the night of September 21st. An appeal was made in the Leader (see this page) on behalf of the proprietors. It must have not have met with much success, as "Neptune" in his letter of the following year (above) describes the bathing boxes as battered wrecks. Interestingly, the appeal made in the Leader is dated November 11th, 1918, the day of the armistice was signed which brought the First World War to its conclusion. Under the notice is part of the Editorial commenting on the armistice.

STORM IN KILKEE.

Loss of Messrs Brann's Bathing Boxes

MUCH sympathy is felt for Messrs J. and T. BRANN for the severe financial loss they have sustained in the complete destruction of Eleven Bathing Boxes, which occurred on Saturday night, September 21st.

To give practical expression to this sympathy a fund has been opened with the object of recouping them for the loss.

Friends and visitors to Kilkee who desire to share in this worthy action might send subscriptions to—

MR J M MULHALL,
Manager Provincial Bank,
Kilkee.

LOCAL COMMITTEE:
Rev Canon Glynn, P P; Rev Canon Blood Smyth, Mr J M Mulhall,
Treasurer—PROVINCIAL BANK.
Subscriptions will be received by this paper.

LIMERICK LEADER.

MONDAY EVENING, NOV. 11, 1918.

The Last Shot

THE last shot has been fired in the world war and the curtain, as a consequence, rings down on the most hideous and horrible drama in human history. Germany has accepted and signed the armistice terms submitted by the Allies and fighting ceased at eleven o'clock this morning. The news of the cessation of hostilities will bring unmingled joy to the hearts of righteous people in every part of the habitable globe. For over four years the work of human slaughter has gone on with a fiendish fury without parallel and on a gigantic scale that appals and staggers the imagination even to contemplate. The loss and havoc and destruction involved in the fearful cataclysm are almost beyond calculation, and are certainly such as can never be fully or adequately repaired. The best that can be hoped for is that new and better standards of right and justice and civilisation will replace those under which the terrible conflict that has drawn to a close was possible. Compensation may to some extent at least be made for the material damage done, but no power on earth can restore the millions of valuable lives that have gone down in the sickening welter of blood that has been deluging Europe since August, 1914. For those who have lost relatives

Peter Stringer marshals his formidable front row, Hayes, Sheehan and Clohessy, with David Wallace giving a hand.

The cup of affliction: Cardiff 2002

THREE-HUNDRED and sixty years ago, the rafters of St Mary's Cathedral rang to the strains of the *Te Deum* to celebrate the great Irish victory over the English in the Battle of Benburb. Rinucinni, the papal legate, presided over this thanking of the Lord for such a rare victory over the ancient enemy. The year was 1646. Fast forward to 26th May 2002, and down the road in St Mary's Church, another choir had planned a similar *Te Deum*. It would come in the form of the recessional Welsh hymn *Bread of Heaven* and without pause, straight into the *Parish Anthem*. That is if Munster had landed the Heineken Cup in Cardiff. Instead, the choir sang Verdi's *Speed Your Journey* from *Nubucco*, its gloomy finale matching the post-match mood:
We have drunk from the cup of affliction
And have shed bitter tears of repentance.

Oh, inspire us, Jehovah, with courage,
So that we may endure to the last.
So that we may endure to the last.

Endure is right. For the sports mad Limerick folk, who in the past decade had seen two All-Ireland's slip away, not to talk of Twickenham, it was in indeed another cup of affliction. Another Holy Grail reached, another Holy Grail snatched away from us at the last minute.

We had set out from Shannon Airport in right form. Sure wasn't it a Protestant wind that had snatched O'Gara's winning kick narrowly past the posts in Twickenham? There'd be no repeat of that with the covered pitch in the Millennium Stadium in Cardiff, and with our Celtic cousins in their thousands to cheer us on against the common enemy from Leicester, the portents were good.

Woody gave us a great gee-up, saying the hurt of Twickenham had not been forgotten, and like de Valera looking into his heart, he saw our time had come. It was rumoured that great jinx on Munster, Richard Harris, was going to stay away. A noted magpie, not alone for Munster but his adopted club Munsters, he met a Limerick man in the toilet before the kick-off at Twickenham who said they were saying novenas in St. Mary's all Friday night praying his plane would be delayed and that he would miss the game.

We looked forward to the pre-match crack, like we had in the swanky, leafy suburbs of Twickenham two years previously. Maybe meet up with a few Welsh fans and hear stories of Garret and Cliff and Phil? Maybe a choir or two and someone quoting Dylan Thomas? Instead, we were greeted with blasts of disco music from the city centre pubs. End of sing-song aspirations, our rendition of "The Isle" could barely be heard above the racket.

A break for chips, and entry into St. Mary Street, showing signs of former grandeur but now like a faded old beauty. A cavalcade of stretch limos sweeps into its broad thoroughfare led by a motor cycle police escort. It was dramatically halted by two stout Welsh mounted policemen. Pedestrians only. We waited with bated breaths to see the occupants emerge. Maybe Bertie and Tony arm in arm off to the match? No. No less a personage than Tony O'Reilly (sorry, Sir Anthony), emerging majestically to be greeted by derisory cheers from Munster gawkers lining the footpaths. We recalled the same ironic cheers when he trotted regally in immaculate gear on to Thomond Park in Dolphin colours. They were playing Shannon in the cup, and the then plain Tony has reminisced of how, before the kick-off, an attempt was made to intimidate them by loud responses to the Rosary emanating from the Parish team's dressing room.

The legendary Jim McCarthy also emerged from the limo. Ahadee, Jim, you ducked past many a Welsh forward, but not this time boy. Tony consulted with the police. "A bit of a misunderstanding maybe, can we be on our way now?" But the Welsh mounties were not for turning.

Nothing for it then but for the beautiful people to shanks mare with the common throng milling towards the stadium. Sir Anthony, in his pin-striped, immaculately tailored suit, his shirt from Penney's was not. Now cast amongst the Dunnes Stores anoraked horde, the slagging was fierce, but he took it all in the best of form. He had little choice.

We sat back in the stadium waiting for the choirs and bands to come on. An ear shattering boom, boom, boom was all we got. A DJ inanely shouted us to know who could cheer the loudest. Imagine, asking us who hoarsed ourselves for either Garryowen, Shannon or Munsters over the years in the Munster Cup, who had goaded Munster on to beat the All Blacks, and cheered Munsters in '93 when they were first from Limerick to land the A.I., imagine asking us could we cheer louder than the Leicester fans.

Mick Galwey holds tough.

Television did not do justice to the unbelievable support given our heroes. If ever a team should have been carried on to victory on a wave of sheer willing on, it was Munster, but sadly it was not enough. The malaise that inexplicably dogged the Munster and national line-outs continued and was to lead to our downfall eventually, Leicester's first try emanating from the frantic to-ing and fro-ing at the back of our line-out. On the practice ground what seemed like a Blackadder Baldrick cunning plan, became unstuck. Our hearts were in our mouths even at our own throw in.

Camped on their line towards the end, and needing a try, we hoped against hope. But deep down somehow we felt it would not come. Years inured to defeat at the final hurdle you see. How many times had we a foot in the door of paradise only to have it slammed in our faces? Even if that boolum Back had kept his hand in his pocket, somehow we knew we were going to be glorious once more in defeat.

In Twickers, we soon got over our disappointment and we mixed, sang and laughed with our conquerors from Northampton. But to be mortally wounded again in such a short time was hard to take, Cardiff we did not paint red. Even the two Paudies, our duo of court jesters, could not get us going. The airport could not come soon enough. If only we knew what was before us.

Utter chaos. It's bad enough to be stranded at an airport at the best of times, but badder a thousand times when your team loses a European Cup for the second time in two years. To paraphrase the character Mary Byrnes from Athlunkard Street, if those in charge were hanged for being an airport authority, they'd have all died innocent.

Imagine a woman airport employee trying to make announcements with a hand megaphone, endeavouring to be heard above the horde sardined into the temporary departure marquee. Saigon was like a meeting of the St Mary's Woman's Sodality compared to it. At the Benediction at that.

We were some of the lucky ones . . . . we thought. We got on our plane after a two hour wait, but then it took the same again before we flew off. We looked out, half expecting to see desperate passengers hanging on to the wings. Some didn't get home until the sun was well up over the Shannon Estuary. The end of a perfect day it was not.

Once again sing the songs of our homeland.
Sing again of the days that are past.
Oh remembrance of joy and of woe.

Peter Stringer crossing the line

Our cup runneth over: Cardiff 2006

'Twas generally agreed that young Stringer,
At passing the ball was a dinger;
Betsen thought the same,
Picked out the wrong lane,
And Peter ducked in for the winner.

Let joy be unconfined, no sleep till morn is past,
Bitter tears are now forgotten, victory is ours at last,
And the tag of gallant losers, confined now to the bin,
As our valiant Munster win the day, our ship at last comes in.

When Bobo scored the opening try, his boot the line it touched,

'Tis the curse of old St Munchin, some said we're surely
   f---d.
O'Neill in Lille, the hand of Back, it seems to be our
   fate,
We're shagged, we're cussed, the game is up, they'll
   bate us out the gate.

Their gander's up, they'll win that cup, they'll find us
   easy mate,
'Tis lonely now in Cardiff's field, for those of little faith.
But Foley cried, rise up, rise up, we shall win the day
Like Sarsfield once, on Limerick's walls, he urged them
   to the fray.

The Bull and Flan, and Paul and all, their response was
   quick and deft,
Like men possessed, they swiftly left, the Basquemen
   soon bereft,
Like panzers to the line bore down, no power on earth
   can shore,
Those men from Mumhan, wired to the moon, sent
   Halsted in to score.

"That Stringer's just a passer," the critics cried en
   masse,
And Betsen, with his deep black eyes, waited for
   expected pass.
But like a young buck rabbit, Pete bolted for the line,
And left the Basqueman, mouth agape, to admire a try
   sublime.

O'Gara rose from bed that morn, his stomach sick and
   sore,
But 'twas nothing to Basque belly aches, as he put over
   score by score.
Spurs claimed a match the previous week because of
   tummy pain,
But O'Gara, 'cause he's Munster, treated his with sheer
   disdain.

In eight years time, we'll celebrate, the Battle of
   Clontarf,
When Brian Boru and his Munster crew, bate the Danes
   into the surf.
And captain Foley, from Brian's home place, Kincora of
   the Brave,
If there, a general would surely be, leading Dalgais in
   the charge.

And as Brodar, the Danish mariner chief, his axe to
   Brian did raise,
A figure in red, he charged the tent, his eyes were all
   ablaze.
'Tis the Bull, 'tis the Bull, band tied round his head, with
   fury he did reek,
And drove the Dane, his axe and all, into the following
   week.

We saw the match in Sunny Beach, in Bulgaria's
   temperate clime,
In company with Munster fans, even some from the dear
   old Isle.
When the camera showed O'Connell Street, a tear or
   two we shed,
The Black Sea for one moment, seemed to turn a shade
   of red.

Oh how we cheered, slapped sun burned backs, and
   partied through the night,
But then the beer was very cheap, €1.40 for a pint.
The Germans even cheered us, hurrah for Deutschland.
You see they thought that Munster was the one in their
   fairland!

Now Biarritz is a lovely place, the beaches are so fine,
Its surfing and its sun-tanned girls, the cuisine is
   sublime.
We've got our burgers, pale white chips, pigs' toes and

58

greasy fry,
And most of all the European Cup, for it the Basques
*   would die.*

And when their life is over, and our team are borne up,
St. Peter he will welcome them, "come in, you've earned
*   that cup."*
And as he goes to shut the gates, our captain says hold
*   on,*
What about the crowd outside, sure them you cannot
*   shun.*

St. Pete he looks, and shouts out loud, and shakes his
*   rugged head,*
"Tis the dozen tribes of Israel, all dressed in brilliant
*   red.*
"The psalms they're singing, about some fields, I've
*   never heard that blast,*
"They can stick their chariot up their arse, we've a new

one got at last."

The Lord appears and gazes on, the throng so big and
*   vast*
And to St. Peter said "tis the Judgment Day at last."
"Oh no, my Lord, 'tis not yet come, 'tis Munster's tribes
*   are here,*
They've come to see their heroes off, and adore their
*   God so dear."*

The Lord was pleased, "ye men of faith, rewards I'll
*   give to you,*
Blessed mansions, virgins, pints are free, for tickets ye'll
*   not queue."*
The red clad horde rushed past the gates, "there's God'
*   it was their cry,*
And raised Paul Connell shoulder high, to the Fields of
*   Athenry."*

All smiles on O'Connell Street.

It's a small thing that dirties a man's shirt

AN English travel writer once wrote in derogatory fashion that it was a game played by stable boys in the south of Ireland. Haughty bridge and solo players look down on it with disdain, but if a head count was made of the amount of people in the city or county who at one time or other tried their hand at the game, '45' stands out as by far the most popular Limerick card game of all time.

There is a legend that the game was introduced here by King William's soldiers during the Siege of Limerick. If true, then the game spans five centuries.

Michael Hogan, the Bard of Thomond, in his wonderful epic, "Drunken Thady" (written in the 19th century) has the first recorded description of a game of '45', played in the early hours of a fateful Christmas Day:

At half-past one the town was silent,
Except a row rais'd in the Island,
Where Thady – foe to sober thinking–
With comrade boys sat gaily drinking!
A table with a pack of cards
Stood in the midst of four blackguards,
Who with the bumper-draught elated,
Dash'd down their trumps, and swore, and cheated!
Four pints, the fruits of their last game,
White-foaming, to the table came;
They drank, and dealt the cards about,
And Thady brought "fifteen wheel out!"
Again the deal was Jack Fitzsimon's,
He turned them up, and trumps were diamonds,
The ace was laid Billy Mara,
And beat with five by Tom O'Hara;
The queen was quickly laid by Thady,
Jack threw the king and douced the lady!
Bill jink'd the game and cried out "Waiter!
Bring in the round before 'tis later"
The draughts came foaming from the barrel;
The sport soon ended in a quarrel;
Jack flung a pint at Tom O'Hara,
And Thady levell'd Bill Mara.
The cards flew round in every quarter,
The earthen floor grew drunk with porter.
The landlord ran to call the Watch,
With oaths half Irish and half Scotch,
The Watch came to the scene of battle,
Proclaiming peace, with sounding wattle;
The combatants were soon arrested,
But Thady got off unmolested.

There is hardly a sporting club, church or charitable organisation in the city or county that has not at one time or other benefited from the proceeds of a '45' Drive. Back in the 1930's and 40's, the famous Sunday afternoon Drives in Athlunkard Boat Club used attract up to seventy tables (420 players), and with a legal limit in force on the amount of prize money that could be given out, span new pianos were given to the winners on occasions. Every available space had to be utilised: the dance hall, clubhouse and even its hallway, to squeeze in the huge crowd.

The Garda Benevolent Fund benefited greatly from the great Drives which took place at three different venues such the Savoy, Cruise's Hotel and Mechanics Institute years ago, and to the present day Mungret A.F.C. and G.A.A. clubhouses still attracts good crowds.

While supermarkets have now put the turkey within range of most households, in the old days to win a turkey at a Drive was a major triumph, and many a grateful family had their Christmas bird supplied through the card playing skills of a parent. During the

World War II rationing, packets of tea were often given as prizes and such was the scarcity of the commodity that it was akin to winning packages of gold-dust.

In the those days, with money so scarce, a win at a drive made a big difference to the weekly income. Players fought for every trick and as a consequence those making mistakes were pounced on and eaten alive.

There is now a big fall off in younger players taking up the game, a result no doubt of the plentitude of money about now, and the fact that TV and videos have driven the card games out of the house. It sets one wondering, then, will the game survive with its falling off in popularity with the younger generation.

The game, to those used to playing it, is fairly uncomplicated. The most popular form is a group of six players, made up of three teams, needing to raise enough tricks to reach 45 and win the game. First to reach three games win the rubber. A jink (reaching 45 without losing a trick) is counted as a game. Best trump is the five, followed by the knave, ace of hearts, etc. with the highest in red and lowest in black being strongest cards.

For beginners, or participants with very modest ability, it is a daunting task to sit in with a group of experienced players, some of whose patience would not extend to making allowance for probationers. A particularly aggressive player devoured beginners in Athlunkard Boat Club without salt to such an extent that he blighted many a burgeoning career in the game.

My late mother Joan was a formidable player and like many of those very adept at the game, had little patience with lesser '45' mortals. One of her partners at one stage, who would be far from fluent in the game, used sometimes pray she'd get few trumps in her hand which would preclude her from making mistakes, thus escaping the wrath of her partner.

Joan, when she retired to Milford House, was somewhat unsettled and I suggested, to help pass the time, that she should play in the weekly '45' game organised for the benefit of the patients. The following week, when enquiring how she was enjoying the game, she stated bluntly she wouldn't be playing anymore. Asked why, she replied that when she played the five the lady next to her put the knave on it and took in the trick.

"But the five beats the knave," claimed Mam.

"Not here it doesn't," said her opponent triumphantly.

On one memorable occasion in a game in St. Michael's Temperance, the best trump was the two of diamonds. "Twouldn't happen in Lourdes," one wit was heard to remark.

Players have their own language in city and county and sexual equality has yet to catch up with game, constant references being made to the low and high man. Just as well the women's libbers of New York, who tried to change the rule of king beating the queen, don't play here.

Many and varied are the expressions used, such as when taking the king off the deck head after robbing, a player will lay it, saying "never pick up a king." Throwing a small trump into the high man is often described as: "tis a small thing that dirties a man's shirt". "I got Susie" means you have the ace of trumps. "You'd get that in Bodyke" describes someone winning a handy trick, and leading the ace after robbing can be followed with the expression "let the dog see the rabbit."

Another popular expression, when the pairs are all forties, or in rubbers, equal with two games each, is "dog eat dog" (madra ith madra as Irishians will say).

Certain cards have their own appellations such as the ten of spades which is called "The Tulla Hearse," or "diamonds are for ladies." The ace of hearts was often referred to as the "Bonham" an expression originating in the county.

Throwing a small trump into the high man is often followed with the expression "for fear of the frost." "A Rathkeale deal" is dealing one card and then four to each player. This, according to the rules printed below, is illegal, two plus three to each person or three plus two to each person being the only two deals allowed.

The act of attempting to let your partner know, by devious facial expressions. or scratching your ear, that you have the five, or do not want him or her to lead, is called "wiring" in the city. This is seriously frowned on and has been the cause of many a row. In Clare, this unsporting method of communication between partners is called "tokens."

While the basic rules are the same all over for the game, minor variations occur in different venues. Of interest is the following set of rules of '45' published by the Limerick Leader in the 1930's:

Cutting for partners: King card is highest and ace the lowest. The parties cutting the lowest play together, have the selection of places, dealing and the choice of cards.

The lowest card deals first: The two lowest being equal, cut again for deal. Two cutters-in are allowed to each table and the right of priority is established by the order in which they have entered the room.

Dealing: In dealing, the cards must be dealt either two to each person or three to each person.

Re-deal: When the pack is found to be imperfect before the trump card is turned. When a card is face up in the pack. When a card is accidentally exposed, through adversary's fault, or under circumstances over which the dealer or his partner has no control.

Loss of deal: Dealing without having the cards cut. Dealing too many or too few cards, if the trump card is turned.

Loss of trick: Leading out of turn, or playing to a card which has been played out of turn. You cannot win with the card played.

Loss of game or bar: 1. Playing too many or too few cards. 2. Playing without robbing, or when you turn the ace, not discarding before you play. 3: Revoking (now called reneging). 4: Improperly putting up the hand. 5: Robbing without the ace in hand. 6: Throwing down hand, or exposing it before game is won, unless you hold the winning cards.

Miscellaneous:
To establish a revoke (renege) the party claiming it must name the trick in which it occurred, previous to examining the cards.

Should the trump card be robbed, it must remain exposed until the first round has been played.

It shall be considered that you rob, when you quit your card and no other card can be substituted.

If a question arises which cannot be disposed of by the rules, a person or persons may be selected by the players, and his or their decision shall be final.

(One rule the above doesn't cover is the long-standing controversy of either having to play a heart on the lead of the ace of hearts, when that suit is not trumps, or withholding it. Many maintain that you need not play a heart, others maintain that you must. Local rules usually apply).

Thinking of what might have been: sitting in Alex Ferguson's seat in Old Trafford.

Did you hear the one about Michael Crowe?

MENTION the name of Michael Crowe to a certain generation in Limerick and it is inevitable that you will be met with a smile. "Aha, the Doc. That chancer. Did you ever hear about the one about the time he . . . . . ."

The genial Limerickman has had many handles put to his name down the years, such as joker, chancer, bluffer, to mention but some.

Sticks and stones may break his bones, but names they never hurt him.

But to many, the Doc is a hero. There are those who will testify that when the going got rough it was to Michael Crowe they turned to help them in their hour of need. A knight in shining armour, with a line of patter that would charm the birds out of the trees.

They say that like packet and tripe, Mick Crowe and fires went together. And that when something annoyed him instead of cursing he'd say "to blazes with it".

Such was his firesome (sorry, fearsome) reputation in that department that if he had been around at the time of the Great Fire of London, chances are that many would have believed he had a hand it in somehow. Or like Nero, that he fiddled while his premises burned.

Talking about giving a dog a bad name . . . . passing the old Fire Brigade premises in Upper Thomas Street, he'd regularly get a blast from the siren and a friendly shout from within: "Where're you off to Mick?

Shannon RFC, winners Munster Junior Cup 1953-54. Back row: B. Prosser, R. McNamara, R. .Keane, C. O'Flynn, G. Ryan, J. O'Halloran, D. Flannery, G. McNamara,E. Browner, P. O'Halloran, A. Sheppard. Centre: G. O'Halloran, J. Ryan, S. McNamara president; F. O'Flynn, capt,; J. Donovan, F. Roche. Front: J. Keane, M. Kirby, T. Creamer, W. O'Shea. Insets: S. Carroll, M. Crowe

Tell us and we'll have one of the tenders standing by." His party-piece was, not surprisingly, "We'll make a bonfire of our troubles".

"People would believe anything about me," said the former serial schoolboy truant, messenger boy, bus conductor, waiter, plane refueller, publican (twelve different locations), castle entertainments manager, window cleaner, showband manager, politician, national G.A.A. fund raiser, rugby, soccer, Gaelic Games player. You name it, the Doc has been there, done it all.

Like the famous local wit, Gurky McMahon, stories abound about the larks of Doctor Crowe, an appellation that has stuck to him over the years. Like Gurky, legends have risen up about the Doc, many true, others

undoubtedly concocted. But that's the trouble when you become a legend, you enter the mainstream of the public domain, and people think they have the right to believe everything they hear about you

But let's hear a true story first. About the time the Doc dressed up as a priest. Manager of Ballynanty Rovers minor team, they were playing Letterkenny in the semi-final of the F.A.I. Cup in Donegal. Sadly they were beaten one-nil. All was not lost, however, as a photograph of their opponents, which previously appeared in the *Donegal Democrat*, contained the picture of one of the team whom Mick got a tip-off was over age. His suspicions were confirmed when after the match two young kids ran on to the pitch to greet the suspect under-age player.

The Doc, ever resourceful, had come prepared. He took his theatrical priest's outfit out of his bag and repaired to the local parish priest's house. He pretended he was back from the States and looking for a family birth register for a friend who was not well. The P.P., beholding to a man of the same calling, opened up the register and there it was in black and white, the offender was two years over age. The Doc took a photo of the register, Balla were awarded the match, and went on to win the cup.

Micheal Crowe was born in Castle View Terrace in Thomondgate in 1930. He has distinct memories of seeing the banner headlines in 1939 announcing the declaration of war. It was not the best of times for the family, especially his father, St. Mary's man Con Crowe. The severe war restrictions on petrol and vehicle travel limitations played havoc with his trade of pig buying. He was a buyer for Shaws and his business suffered accordingly. Mick's mother May, helped out with a huckster shop in Glentworth Street.

Now living in that street, young Michael became an altar server in the nearby Dominican Church. There he brought off his first major jape. At Midnight Mass one Christmas Eve, he proudly led the recessional procession down the main aisle, holding the crucifix aloft. His instructions were to wheel left and head for the aisle containing the shrine to Our Lady of Limerick. Unfortunately, the back of the church was packed, the crowd, including some of his grinning pals, were slow to part, and undaunted, he kept going towards the main entrance. Somebody opened the door, and he led the procession, servers, white-robed friars, Prior and all, out into the freezing night, on to the square in Baker Place, around Tait's Clock, back in, and down the main aisle again.

Unfortunately, the Prior was not too impressed and his services were dispensed with.

His early schooling was in St. Philomena's. And who became his best pal there? Richard Harris, no less. Two boyos if ever there were two. God help their teachers. "Even at that early age, he was up to his antics," said Mick in his recall of Harris. "Later on, when we went to the Crescent, he was up to all kinds of larks, like leaving chewing gum on the teacher's Mr. Glasheen's chair. He was constantly in hot water."

Possibly in anticipation of his future career, Harris was at his best when attending the pictures. "He'd stick his legs over the Gods in the Lyric and his comments brought down the house. His speciality was taking the mickey in the famous Fitzpatrick travelogues. One night Limerick was featured and as James A. was fading out bidding his farewell to the City of the Violated Treaty and the brave women who took on the Williamites, Harris shouts out: "They were all pregnant as well!" Needless to say he brought down the house, and was promptly ejected, Mick recalled.

Michael could not stand the strict discipline in the Crescent at the time and abhorred the use of the strap. "I decided to go mooching and for a year and a half I was out on gull regularly. I then went to St. Munchin's, in Henry Street, and mitched there for two and half years. One day my father met the principal, Fr. Dan Gallagher, and asked him how I was getting on. "I don't think Michael has been with us for some time," said the puzzled principal.

They went in search of him and trapped him in St. Michael's Temperance snooker hall, his father at one door and Fr. Gallagher at the other. "I got a few fine clips across the ear from my father and Fr. Dan as well, but I deserved all I got."

How did he get away with it for so long? "Well, my father used walk with me to the main gate, and when he was gone, I'd double back and make down the lane."

Crescent and St. Munchin's Colleges turned out many priests, doctors and solicitors over the years. What about messenger boys? There was one. Put up your hand Michael Crowe! Yes, he joined the ranks of that distinguished body at fourteen years of age working for Prionsias Mac Giolla Losgaigh (Frank Glasgow, one-time mayor) men's outfitters in Bedford Row. The Doc reminisces:

"He (Frank) was a great Irishian. Everything was *Leabhar Ghaeilge anseo*. My first instructions were to *faigh an scuab agus glan an fhuinneog*! One of the calls I had to make was to St. Mary's Park where I collected weekly instalments on the never-never. There were some great characters down there and I got to know the people well. This stood me in good stead when I opened the Dalcassian singing lounge in Nicholas Street."

What was it like being one of the legendary messenger boys? "I can tell you, you learned more from them than you would at a school of economics. Some of them would buy and sell you. We were paid a pittance and we had to use our initiative to supplement our miserable wages. We'd meet up at the end of Rose's Avenue in the Ennis Road and one would swap say, a pork chop for a bunch of rhubarb, that type of thing. I'd often pick up things like a neck tie in the shop, do a deal and would arrive home with a few lamb chops to my mother.

"Some years back I organised a reunion of messenger boys and we had a great night out in City Hall. I got a loan of one of the famous bikes from Noel Hannon at the top of Upper Cecil Street and the Mayor, Gus O'Driscoll, who used run a lot of errands for his father when he was young, cycled down the main corridor on it!"

Another appellation that the Doc could be bestowed with is *raconteur extraordinaire*. Sit back and listen to

Hoary veterans team ferried from Barrington's pub, 1989, to Priory Park: Back: Dan O'Mahony (physio), Mick Crowe, Denis Keogh, Sean Healy, John English, Jimmy Duhig, Jim Mulcahy, Paschal Madden, Arthur Sheedy. Front: Willie O'Carroll, Liam (Tailo) Ryan, Stephen Healy, Peter Hayes, Vincent McElligott.

some of the tales:

"I must tell you a funny story about a life-like fully clothed dummy which stood inside the shop entrance in Glasgow's. I was playing juvenile with Shannon against Thomond in the cup final and a character called Wiggers Mac bet me a fiver Thomond would win. I never saw a fiver in my life but took a chance and took him on. We won and fair play to Wiggers he arrived down in his horse and car with the fiver. "Would you throw in that old dummy there" he says and I said 'twas all the one to me and off he goes with it. I believe Frank never missed the dummy for a long time and side-stepped the empty space where it stood each morning as if it was still there. I met him when I came back from England and he says *cad mar gheall ar an arigid?* He settled for two pounds."

The 1950's was an era of huge deprivations and like thousands of his fellow countrymen, Mick set sail for England, his fare paid for Wigger's fiver. There he worked as a bus conductor, breakfast chef and waiter. When he came home after a few years he togged out again with Shannon R.F.C. and Paddy O'Driscoll tipped him off about a job refuelling with Esso in Shannon. He worked there with the immortal rugby legend Tom Clifford.

"Tom was one of the most genuine and caring persons I ever met. I got into trouble one time, when bringing the wages to the lads when working nights. There was a big game of poker going on in the emigration centre and being a compulsive gambler, I sat in for a few hands. And stupidly I lost all the wages. I was facing ruin, but next morning Tom took me into the Ulster Bank where he knew the manager and borrowed £800 in his name. The lads were paid and he made me promise I'd never gamble again, which I never did. Needless to say I paid him back over the years, I will never forget what he did for me.

"I overheard Tom getting a phone call one day from the legendary Australian rugby player, Nick Shaheedy.

Nick, noted for his training methods like running up a mountain with a sheep under his arm, had famously tapped Noel Murphy when playing for the Lions and Tom says to him, "you were a bold boy Nick." Nick replies: "I learned that from you Clifford."

1958 was the year which saw the start of the Doc's career as an entrepreneur. He spent a lot of time down St. Mary's way, playing rugby for Shannon and soccer for Star Rovers, and put his eye on a run-down pub in Nicholas Street called the Dalcassian. On enquiries, he found that he could rent it for £4 a week from the owner, Agnes Dinneen. She required a down payment of £16, a month's rent in advance. "That took all my assets and I had to borrow the price of six barrels of stout from my Aunt, Mrs. Griffin, the undertakers. I got a float from Georgie Sullivan, a few crates of lemonade from Willie Grimes."

Shortly afterwards Doc bought out the pub for the princely sum of £16. "I told her if I did well I'd be good to her, which I was."

Six years later in 1964, Doc sold the pub for £12,800, the equivalent then of five new semi-detached houses.

The Dalcassian became famous as Limerick's first singing lounge. Limerick's top organist, John A. Enright, played classics in the early part of the night on an organ that the proprietor paid £700 for. Such top musicians as Donie Collins and Austin Graham played later on in the night. Frances Condell, the eminent Mayor, was a frequent visitor.

"There was a galaxy of local talent such as Fongo Ryan, Mike Sheehy, Nan Collopy, Katie Bullman, Molly Yelverton, and many more, all backed by Matthew Sheedy on the accordion. Joe Neiland, Mick Yelverton, Christy Halloran, all members of the Limerick Operatic Society, used gives us gems from the operas. Coppa Storan and his wife Nellie would make a grand entrance singing 'Sugar in the Morning' and everyone would join in."

Some of the characters around at the time wouldn't

Helping Frankie Flynn sing 'The Isle' at the testimonial with Denis Law.

be the type that would be familiar with the parlour of the nearby St. Mary's Convent. "Would you believe it, I never had a row in the pub. I was on great terms with the Star Rovers, Dalcassian and Island United lads and if there was the smallest hint of trouble they would make their presence felt. I laid down standards from the start which were adhered to."

A tough character with a fearsome reputation walked in one evening. Mick had been warned not to serve him more than one drink. Likened to a desperado in a Western film, he burst in the swing doors and demanded an effin pint.

"I pulled him for his language and refused to serve him. There was a crowd of the lads in at the time and they smelled the gunsmoke. Like you'd see in a Western, they all started to drift into the back. Your man says to me, d'you see that barrel there? Yes says I, and over he goes, lifts it and slams it down on the counter. At the time I thought it was empty but realised afterwards it was full.

"I vaulted the counter and taking my life in my hands ordered him out. As he went out the door he half turned and I got my retaliation in first, managing to push him out onto the footpath. A bus was passing at the time and mounted the footpath sending our friend through Hinchey's butcher's window pane next door. The butcher, thinking his shop was being attacked, used his mallet on the head of your man who at this stage didn't know what was happening.

"A big crowd had gathered around at this stage and I

made a great impression when I shouted at the blood-covered figure: 'try that again and I'll really lose my temper with you.'

"I basked in the glory of that for a long time. Our friend was in hospital in later years and when I went to see him he says, 'Mick, what did you hit me with that day?' When I told him it was the butcher that did it, he said I can effin well die happy now. Incidentally, it took three of us to lift the barrel off the counter."

"There were some great wits. There was a group of hard drinkers who'd give me most of their wages and dole money at the start of the weekend and by Monday afternoon they'd be on the book. There was a right crowd of them in one Monday morning nursing the last of their paid for drinks, and I was fearful of leaving the bar in case some of them would decide on some self-service. As luck would have it, three Yanks walked into the bar and the boys rubbed their hands in anticipation of a soft touch.

"You'll have a drink on the house," I said to the Yanks in my best Irish hospitality voice. They had three glasses of Guinness.

"A character called Boots Cleary, oozing charm, engaged the Yanks in conversation and found out the group were from Texas, being reminded that it was the biggest State in the U.S.

'How's John Wayne getting' on,' said Boots and the Yank said he was in Hollywood.

'Is he your favourite actor?' he was asked. 'Ah no, replied Boots, Wayne wouldn't hold a candle to Rin-Tin-Tin.' The Yanks fell about the place laughing and asked Boots if he would like a drink. 'I might,' says Boots, 'and the lads might like one too.' The call came to seventeen pints.

"Boots kept the blarney coming, admitting that while America was indeed a powerful country how could they compare it to ours, a country where lambs made jam, lions made tea, foxes made mints, birds made custard, and donkeys made chips. A few of the lads then gave a few bars. The Yank eventually called three rounds. Boots was the hero of the hour."

Most of his customers had nicknames, like Gully Kelly, Pigeon Roche, Barrell Mac, Tex Griffin, Wabbler Gavin, Skeff Sheehan, Eyepole, etc. "If you called them by their real name, they'd look around to know who was being called."

Fongo Ryan was singing a Matt Munroe number called "Walk Away" one night when he cracked on the high notes. He got some flak from the crowd, and he apologised, saying he was having trouble with the organist. "John Enright got up from the organ, gathered his music and walked out, never to return," Mick recalled.

The Doc got into trouble with Canon Lee once. A horse called *Canabalee* dropped dead in the National and on the Sunday morning Boots Cleary told a few women in the pub wasn't it sad about Canon Lee. "Wha's up with him," they enquired. "He dropped dead yesterday," was the terse reply. The story spread like wildfire.

"The Canon arrived in on Monday morning and accosted me saying the rumour had come from the pub," recounted Mick. "I had to explain to him that it was a misunderstanding about *Canabalee* and he took it in great part."

Sport played a big part in the life of Michael Crowe, and like most things he turned his hand to, he made a success of it. He won Munster Junior Cup with Shannon in 1954 and playing in the club's first senior cup match, against Sunday's Well, kicked two long range penalties, his side's only tally.

"Dan Daly, their out-half, played molly-bawn with us that day and I bought a few of his famous dummies. They gave us a big drubbing and one of the Flynn brothers remarked that I bought more dummies than was in Burton's window!"

In soccer, he was capped for Ireland at junior level, uniquely playing at centre forward and in goal and played goal for Limerick at senior level. He played with Star Rovers for several seasons and also Island United.

He had a famous falling out with Star. Or should we say Star with him. Seemingly the night before a Munster Junior Cup match, he refused to serve two of the Star players and the Doc, top goal scorer for the club that season, was told his services were not required when he turned up in Pa Healy's next morning for the match.

"Micky Arthurs, with whom I played rugby with Shannon, was playing with the opposition, Ennis. They were short so I obliged him by togging out for the Clare side to make a match of it."

Needless to say, the Doc was subject to some hefty tackles and volatile abuse from the sidelines. "To rub salt into their wounds, I scored the wining goal even though we had only nine players. Everyone knew I was illegal turning out for Ennis, but Star's pride was badly dented."

Now there was trouble in the camp. Star mentors were furious at what they saw as an act of treachery, further compounded by the fact that the opposition were invited back to the Dal. for soup and sandwiches. The parish lads decided not alone to boycott the pub but to slap a picket on it as well!

"None of my regular customers would pass the picket and I was facing an empty pub that night. I put my thinking cap on and I called one of the organisers. 'No hard feelings, here's a fiver, get the lads a drink over in the Ramble Inn.' The boys were mightily impressed, there was a quick meeting. 'Ah, he's not the worse of them, we'll have the drink in the Dal.'

Picket lifted, and they had a mighty sing-song with the Ennis lads.

"Fair play, Star accepted their defeat that day, and put no objection in against Ennis, who were beaten in the next round," recounted Mick.

Ahadee now. What about the fires Mick? Mention of his name in any hostelry in town usually meant someone shouting out "Fire! Fire!" The jokers went to town. After a funeral one night the Doc was in the company of Tom Clifford in Gerry O'Dea's pub and he asked Tom to hand him down his change from the counter. Tom obliged but instead of coin, handed the Doc six boxes of matches!

The year Michael went for the Council he was making a speech and someone in the crowd shouted up "You have two votes anyway Doc." "Yourself and the wife?" Mick shouted down. "No, Maguire and Patterson," was the reply.

It all started with the Imperial Hotel, which stood at the corner of Catherine Street and Roche's Street, which in 1966 Mick had purchased for £14,000. A few years later a disastrous fire gutted the building and the legend was born. "What harm, I was in Blackpool playing squash with, ironically, the Chief Fire Officer there, when the fire occurred. I told the ballhoppers that yes, I had burned it down with a 72 hour candle while I was abroad! All I got from the insurance was £8,000 because it could be partly rebuilt. I took down the sign and set up in Ford's in Carey's Road."

Another fire was to follow in the garage attached to his house. The garage contained a big stock of trading stamps, redeemable for funds for Cork's Pairc ui Chaoimh, for which the Doc was chief organiser. The stamps were completely destroyed. "This of course, added greatly to the legend and there was all sorts of stories flying about skulduggery on my part. The facts were simple: one of the kids put out ashes into the garage which were smouldering and this started the fire. A gym I had in William Street was damaged in another fire but that had started upstairs in a restaurant. Of course I was blamed for that too. I didn't care, people believed what they wanted to and I agreed with them and left them off."

You could say a lot of things about Michael Crowe, but you could never accuse him of not having a sense of humour. "I was going up Glentworth Street one day, hurrying and looking at my watch (a ploy he used when creditors were after him) when Jim Kemmy called me. 'There's someone in the White House I want you to meet.' I said I was in a hurry but he said it wouldn't take long and lo and behold who was inside but Frank McCourt."

They both reminisced about the time they used play in the Long Meadow in the People's Park but as the old Limerick saying went, the famous author never asked Mick if he had a mouth on him. "Making my departure, I congratulated him on the success of *Angela's Ashes* and added "I left more ashes in my wake than you ever did and never got a penny out of it."

Mick married Lilly Flanagan, a legendary nurse in her day in Barrington's and a winner of the coveted Curtin medal, awarded to the nurse of the year. "A tall, dark-eyed, willowy beauty," broadcaster David Hanley described her. As a youthful patient in Barrington's, David fell under her spell. So did Mick, and they were married in 1957, going to on to have a fine family of seven children. Two of their sons, David and Niall, immortalised Lily's name in New York, naming their pubs after her.

A ballhopper can be described as one who stirs thing up and then departs leaving chaos in his wake. A perfect appellation for the Doc: he was the main man in the Ballhoppers' Corner during the great soccer days of the Markets Field. You thought you might have got the better of the Doc but he'd wait his chance, especially if you were in Kilkee or some place else for the weekend. And you'd arrive home on Sunday night to find a few tons of sand, or a few hundred blocks of cement, perched in your driveway.

He was caught once. A joker phoned on behalf of a well known detective asking to meet Mick outside the *Cork Examiner* office in O'Connell Street. The prankster did the same to the detective and both victims arrived outside the office to discover they had been had. A few days later the joker arrived home from work to

Peter Hayes, subject of' 'This is Your Life' in Barrington's Pub.

find that three tons of quick drying cement had hardened in his driveway!

A well known gravedigger in Mount St. Laurance's used get a laugh pretending to measure the Doc and asking when he'd be coming up to him. "He was at it one night in a pub. I was on the City Council at the time and I said to the lads did ye hear the news? 'There's a crowd looking for planning permission to open a crematorium and I think I'll be voting for it. And it's one fire I won't be blamed for.' Your man left me alone after that."

A decrepit busker, who used cover his ear with his hand as if he didn't like his own singing, used entertain at the Markets Field during the great days. One Sunday, as he usually did, he gave his cap to the ever-obliging Doc to make the collection amongst the crowd. It was after Mick's narrow defeat in the election, and also the morning after the Eurovision contest.

"You had tough luck in the Eurovision last night," said the Doc to the entertainer, a sally which brought a howl from the crowd. There was even a bigger cheer when your man riposted: "Ah yes Mr. Crowe, you'd know all about being beaten by a few votes."

What would surely have been his greatest of all japes was foiled at the last minute. The Doc hired two lads with a van to go into the Dominican Church, take possession of the most treasured Our Lady of Limerick statue and transport it to the Augustinians. "If ye're stopped, say that the bishop wants the statue to be revered in other churches," the Doc told them. Unfortunately (or fortunately would be more like it) Brother Anthony was in the vicinity, smelled a rat, and the jape was aborted.

Mick stood for the Dail in the bye-election after Donogh O'Malley's sudden death in 1968, won by Des O'Malley. Canvassing in the Doon area with his three young sons, they called to the convent where the reverend mother called all the community and staff together in the parlour to meet the politician. After giving a spiff as to why they should vote for him, he asked the gathered community if they had any questions. All kept their heads bowed demurely and the reverend mother turned to him and said "you can be assured that you'll get all our votes here Mr. O'Malley."

The Doc's final rally was to be outside the O'Connell Monument, but unfortunately it clashed with Fine Gael's wind-up as well. He booked out every marching band in town to foil the opposition and cancelled them that Saturday afternoon, too late for his rivals to book them.

"Thousands of Fine Gael supporters led by Gerry Sweetman marched up O'Connell Street to their rally. I was waiting with my supporters at the corner of Roche's Street and at the head of Gerry Cusack's jazz band we stepped in front of the Fine Gael contingent and marched towards the monument. Bystanders looked in amazement at the crowd that was following me, saying my God look at the crowd supporting the Doc. I met Sweetman in South's afterwards, he was like a divil. I pulled 2,000 votes, but not enough to get elected."

The Doc was more successful in the local elections in 1974 and was elected to the City Council, garnering a splendid vote of 870 first preferences. "There were some characters on the Council at that time such as Steve Coughlan, Mick Lipper and Jim Kemmy. If things were quiet I'd stir things up by turning to Stevie and whispering 'did you hear Kemmy is being financed from Moscow!' Things could get acrimonious at times at the meetings but they'd go off and have a few pints together afterwards."

Not for the first time, the Doc walked into it, at a meeting of the Society for Prevention of Cruelty to Animals. "I was deputising for the Mayor and the meeting was in the George Hotel. When I went up to the podium I remarked on the huge crowd present, saying 'you couldn't swing a cat here.' There was a dead silence. I wasn't asked back again."

He caused a sensation when he resigned from the Council after just two years. It was unheard of at the time for such a thing to happen. "There were no increments that time, and it was hugely expensive to be an independent. I ran into trouble financially and even had my electricity cut off. Ironically, previously I had got some of my constituents reconnected after pleading with the E.S.B. Also, as an independent, I felt powerless and asked the city manager, Mr. MacDiarmada at a meeting what powers I had, if any. He replied none really, but maybe I could act in an advisory capacity. I asked him would you act on my advice and he replied not really. That finished me and I resigned."

How did he get the appellation Doc? "We were in Germany with Ballynanty in the European Youths Cup

Sporting legends all: at the launch of Mick Crowe's testimonial match in 1998: Joe O'Mahony, Pat Hartigan, Al Finucane, Colm Tucker, Mick Crowe.

when Larry Fitzgerald started to introduce me as Dr. Crowe. The German coach, Hans Masheric had taken ill in the hotel and would you believe it my name was called over the address system to attend the stricken man. I examined him and prescribed some aspirin. He recovered quickly and was profuse in his thanks."

Despite massive objections and huge protest marches, Barrington's Hospital was closed in 1988 during the fiscal rectitude reign of the late Charlie Haughey. At the time, Mick Crowe, once more in the pub business, rescued several items from the hospital, and had them installed in his pub in Broad Street which he re-named simply Barrington's. These items included the operating table, x-ray equipment and a suspended

bed from the ceiling with half a male torso strapped into it complete with a notice underneath: *I'm not half the man I used to be.*

"Did we have a lot of fun there," recalled the Doc, who was elected President of St. Mary's R.F.C. during his tenure. "Valerie Cox made a programme on the pub for the Pat Kenny show and when she arrived I greeted her in my doctor's white coat and stethoscope. From the door marked A & E. arrived three characters, brothers Stephen and Sean Healy and Dutch Mac. Dutch ordered three pints, three small ones and six packages of Afton Major. 'Take it out of that,' he says to me, proffering his medical card.

The RTE researcher watched with fascination and

when the programme was aired, Pat Kenny, in his normally serious mode, cast doubts on the story and the authenticity of Mick's role as a doctor. "I'm not so sure," replied Valerie, "they all kept calling him Doc."

Peter Hayes, one of the famous brothers from Flag Lane in the Abbey, all seven of whom played rugby with St. Mary's, was another character who frequented the pub. Hearing that Peter had received his fifty year medal with the Arch Confraternity, the Doc decided to have a *This Is Your Life* evening in the pub. He persuaded the director of the confraternity to come down as one of the guests. Another guest was Dobbin the horse. Peter had driven such a horse for many years for Cantrell & Cochrane and where Mick resurrected it nobody knows. Anyway, when the horse was brought in it brought down the packed house and Peter became very emotional.

"Peter used tell me a story about when he was in England his landlady persuaded him to join the Salvation Army. He often recalled one of their rallying cries which was : 'Give the bible to the preacher and give your heart to Jesus. Alleluia.' I got Peter, the gentlest of characters, to repeat this during the programme and being carried away, he finished it up shouting *Allefuchingluia* with his arms outstretched to tremendous cheering. Who had just arrived in at the time but the director of the Confraternity and when Peter spotted him he nearly died."

In all, Mick owned at one time or other twelve public houses. He spearheaded the campaign to save Mungret College for the people, successfully raised funds to bring the Kerry football team around the world in 1970, managed Bunratty and other castles belonging to Shannon Development, and was marketing director with Limerick AFC and PRO. Been there, did it all.

Many of the players of the great Limerick soccer teams of the 1970's and 1980's have stories in connection with the Doc. They are all in accord regarding his generosity and character, not to mention his larks.

"We were playing in Sligo once and he made his car available to the team," recalled Vinny Quin, who had a long and successful career with Limerick. "Unfortunately it was involved in a crash and apprehensively the lads called up Mick to tell him the bad news. "Anyone hurt," he enquired. When told no, the Doc replied, "what are ye worried about then."

"If it was anyone else they'd be fuming," Vinny said. "It was typical of the man. It's unknown how many people he helped down the years who were in trouble of one kind or another."

A man who would testify to that is Tom Hickey, who had a TV shop in Parnell Street. "Mick bought television sets for several people down on their luck and I delivered them under the strict understanding that I was not to say who the benefactor was," he recalled.

Limerick were playing in Athlone one day and the team dropped into the Prince of Wales Hotel for a bite to eat. The place was red carpeted and packed with dignitaries for a function which the late Cardinal Conway was to attend.

The Cardinal swept in and Mick said to his companions, Andy McEvoy, Joe O'Mahony and Kevin Fitzpatrick: "There goes my old friend."

Knowing his reputation, the lads wouldn't believe him.

"Would you shut up out of that Crowe," said Kevin Fitzpatrick.

"I'll bet you he'll say hello Mick Crowe," said the Doc.

Fitzy took him on.

The Doc joined the queue of dignitaries and lined up to kiss the Cardinal's ring, with the lads looking on bemusedly. When he knelt down he whispers to the Cardinal "I'm Michael Crowe from Limerick."

When the Doc stood up the cardinal says out loud: "and how are ye all down in Limerick Michael!"

Limerick United scoring ace Des Kennedy recalls Crowe's astuteness. "I was giving him a lift one Sunday morning before a match when a driver from Dublin ran into me in O'Connell Street. There wasn't much damage but he insisted it was my fault and said he had a car load of witnesses to prove it. Crowe spotted a well known character way ahead of us and calling him said did he see the car hitting us. Your man copped on, said he did, and would be a witness if we wanted. The Dubliners scooted off straight away."

Such was the esteem in which the Doc was held, one of the last of the great Limerick's characters, that a group got together in 1988 and organised a testimonial match in Clifford Park. It was a challenge between Manchester United legend Denis Law's team and Kerry's Mick O'Dwyer's selection, with many household names in soccer, rugby, Gaelic and hurling taking part, testimony to the high regard in which the Doc was held nationally. True to the flamboyance of the Doc's character, Denis Law arrived in style, landing in the middle of the playing pitch in a helicopter. A great night was had by all and was a fitting tribute to Mick, a great sport, an appellation that sums up perfectly the character of the man called the Doc.

Paying tribute on local radio beforehand was rugby legend Tony Ward. "He (Mick) is the epitome of the type of sportspeople you meet in Limerick. When Eoin Hand's testimonial did not do so well in Dublin for various reasons, the Doc organised another testimonial and dinner here which was a huge success. Typical of the generosity of the man. Why he was never elected Mayor of the city I do not know."

Also paying tribute was another sporting legend, Al Finucane, who gives us the final story in this saga of the man called Doc. "Back in the 1970's, Limerick were returning from a European Cup match and in Heathrow we met up with the famous Benefica team who were also in transit. We chatted with those who had English and they asked some of us to swap club badges. Unfortunately we didn't have any.

"We noticed the Doc deep in conversation with none other than the legendary Eusabio. As our flight was being called, both came towards us with the Doc proudly wearing a Benefica badge and Eusabio proudly sporting a Pioneer pin!"

Eoin Hand, forever associated with the glory years of Limerick United, wrote for the testimonial: "When I came to Limerick first, I heard stories of Mick Crowe even before I met him. He is a man with the common touch, and to use an old Limerick saying, I, and a lot of other people, have great time for him. He is a legend in his lifetime."

And so say all of us.

When a corpse was hung in St Mary's Cathedral

A STARTLING revelation has in recent times been made that about 1554 the corpse of Edmund Sexton (a favourite of King Henry VIII), was disinterred after his burial in St Mary's Cathedral and lay hanging for three years above the ceiling of the chancel.

The body, minus the amputated right hand, which was left lying in the tomb, was discovered by a fleeing felon who hiding himself above the church, made the grisly discovery.

This extraordinary piece of 16th century history was garnered from the notebook of Sexton's nephew, also named Edmund, discovered amongst ancient Limerick papers in the National Library by Dr Colm Lennon, Dept of Modern History, Maynooth.

Dr Lennon, in a fascinating lecture to member of the Thomond Archaeological Society, threw new insights into Limerick families of the 16th and 17th centuries and the tenuous position of Protestants during the days of the Reformation.

Dr Lennon, whose research on the martyred Bishop Richard Creagh led him to do further research on the Limerick papers, revealed that Sexton in his notebook wrote that the sacrilegious act of hanging his grandfather's corpse in the cathedral was perpetrated because Sexton the Elder had embraced the Reformation. In a letter to the Dublin Government. he uttered the suspicion that his grandfather's physician had been procured by his enemies to bleed him to death because "he had received the gospel."

The perpetrators of the disinterment, all Catholics, were named as Pierse White, described as Sexton's brother-in-law; Alderman Christopher Creagh, and Edward White, the organist at the cathedral.

Edmund Sexton the Elder, introduced into Henry VIII court as a young man, so impressed the King that he made him a server of his chamber, charged with responsibility for table arrangements of guests. On his return to Limerick in 1535 Sexton was made Mayor by order of Henry, despite the fact that it was normally the bailiff who attained that office. More importantly the King, at the dissolution of the monasteries, handed over the abbeys, priories and lands in possession of the religious orders to Sexton.

While there would have been huge resentment at what was then described as the use of crafty means to gain these highly valuable possessions, and later on his embracement of the Protestant religion, Dr Lennon said that the fact that Sexton's Gaelic origins (Seasnáin of Thomond) may also have caused prejudice against him by patrician Limerick families, which was to lead eventually to the grisly desecration of his corpse.

It was a tough time being a member of the minority Protestant religion in Limerick in those times, and especially for Edmund Sexton, being in the possession of the spoils of the monasteries. The constant antagonism of his fellow-citizens was stepped up on his conversion to Protestantism during the reign of Henry's son, Edward VI.

It was also a period of huge political turmoil and when Sexton switched allegiance from the Fitzgerald's to the Butlers, his newly built house in Corbally was attacked by James, the Earl of Desmond, who expelled him with violence, seized his goods and produce worth 500 marks and retained the property.

St. Mary's Cathedral and King John's Castle

On Edmund's death around 1554, his son Stephen became head of the family: his older brother George had died in extraordinary circumstances in England when he was hit on the head by a flying cowlstaff that had been thrown after him by a woman at Charing Cross.

If Edmund had a tough time, Stephen's lot was no easier. There was nothing superficial about Stephen's adherence to the Reformation, said Dr Lennon, as he collected books on all aspects of the Protestant religion. Stephen was one of a tiny coterie of Limerick Protestants which was described by the Jesuit papal commissary David Wolfe in 1574 as "seven or eight young men who embrace the Lutheran leprosy more to please the Lady Elizabeth than for any other reason."

Stephen was Mayor in 1574, and he died prematurely in 1594, according to his son Edmund (from whose notebook and documents the family history was gleaned), "because of persecution at the hands of the dominant Limerick recusant community, and because of the great grief occasioned him through harassment over his claims to the former monastic property in the city."

On his father Stephen's death, Edmund the Younger succeeded to the family estates. He was educated at Oxford University and the Inns of Court in London, a fact which was to stand him in good stead due to the many litigations he was to face throughout his lifetime regarding the properties requisitioned by his grandfather. It was he who compiled the notebook which contains a chronicle of the family's history including the account of his grandfather's disinterment. The picture that emerged is that of struggle for survival.

In Edmund's view, he was a member of a persecuted minority (Protestant) and in order to preserve his identity as part of one whose religious and political loyalties were firmly focussed on the State, he forged social and professional links more with the New English community in the North Munster region than with the Old English citizenry, which made him more isolated from the municipal mainstream.

Sexton was very proud of his citizenship of Limerick and though frequently at odds with the Corporation over titles to property and other matters, he seems to have played a full part in civic administration. He served as Mayor of Limerick on at least four occasions, mostly as substitute for debarred Catholics, primarily in order to save the Corporation from the threat of dissolution, which had occurred several times in Waterford due to religious dissidence in the council.

Edmund married Joan, daughter of Justice James Gould, a Church of Ireland member, and the couple had 17 children, between 1597 and 1620, six of whom died in infancy. Enclosed within this very small world of North Munster Protestantism, Sexton aspired to control the destinies of his family. He attempted to arrange weddings for them where possible within the restricted Church of Ireland community, but at least some of his children were wedded to Catholics.

Sexton reiterates through his journal the "malice of the majority towards himself and his ancestors only for . . . religion and adhering to the State, as well as experiencing their 'general hatred against all possessors of the true religion.' "

He quotes Psalm 129 as an example of the characterisation of the sentiments of the citizens of Limerick towards him: "Ever since I was young, my enemies have persecuted me cruelly, but they have not overcome me. They have cut deep wounds in my back and made it like a ploughed field. But the Lord, the righteous one, has freed me from slavery."

The spoils of the monasteries granted to his grandfather lay at the root of Edmund's problems as the leading councillors of the city harboured bitter resentment at the Sexton acquisition of these valuable lands and properties. Edmund spent a great amount of time and money (in an age of primitive transportation he was required to travel to Dublin regularly soliciting support) in defending his rights through the courts and his training as a lawyer stood him in good stead here.

Even though James I eventually issued a patent letter confirming full possession of the properties, Edmund was frequently obstructed in access to the friary by Corporation workers who intruded into the possessions and his privileges as the successor of the priors were denied and called into question.

Despite the hatred and harassment he met with, Sexton remained a very proud and loyal citizen of Limerick. He vaunted the municipal achievements of the borough of Limerick which culminated in the charter of incorporation in 1609, and his family's participation in urban life. His loyalty to the corporation in acting as chief magistrate at times when central government was insisting on religious conformity ensured the city's immunities and privileges were maintained.

When the custom's rights of the municipality were under threat in 1608, Sexton, as mayor and a trained lawyer, travelled with James Galway as agent of Limerick to the royal court in London to plead the case for retention of income. His lavish hosting of Lord Deputy Falkland at his house in Gurtenfluch during the latter's visit to the city was important in presenting the civic community in a favourable light to the chief governor.

Vindication of his rights as landlord of former abbey lands precluded a return of monks and friars. At a time of increasingly open Roman Catholic re-organisation in the 1610's and 1620's, and fearful of a recurrence of the revolt of 1603 when James I took the throne, and when friars repossessed churches and priories, Edmund was ever vigilant for the re-entry of friars in their former possessions. Thus he took part in the implementation of the regulations against mass-houses in the city: he supported the President of Munster's campaign to

Chancel in the cathedral with the monument to the Earl of Thomond.

curtail Catholic worship. He had security put in place over St John's Church and the family tomb in the Cathedral which had to be preserved from intrusion of the Creagh family.

Sexton had an extensive library, 40 per cent of which included books of divinity, and his education in Ireland, Oxford and London, had inculcated a breadth of learning and knowledge which become clear from the catalogue of his library.

Sexton's hopes for the transmission of his beliefs through a consolidated family inheritance in Limerick city and its environs were severely dented before his death. It was apparent to him that a Catholic resurgence in the later 1620's was threatening the Protestant holding within the city and amongst his own kinsfolk a pattern of deaths and marrying out disrupted his plans.

The death of his own son Stephen in 1628 at the age of 31 was a blow from which he may never have recovered.

Before his death in 1637, Edmund Sexton had to endure indignities which were reminiscent of the events surrounding his grandfather's demise and some extraordinary scenes were witnessed in the vicinity of his death-bed.

According to evidence in a trial in the court of Castle Chamber later that year, two Protestant clergymen, Ralph Fursman and Roger Hayes were denied admission to the dying Edmund by his wife, Joan, and some of his children, who claimed that he had been converted to Roman Catholicism by the ministry of some priests and friars.

Fursman did eventually with "much shoveing",

force an entry into Sexton's house but was interrupted by loud cries and curses such as "a pox confound ye" and "English doggs" as he tried to pray with Edmund.

The following day the Anglican bishop of Limerick, accompanied by some ministers, arrived at the sickbed to be told by Edmund (according to later evidence) "with teares . . . I knowe not what they have done unto mee but still in heart I am a Protestant, and do desire to live and die."

Sexton's wife Joane, raising the "Irish cry" and clapping her hands from an upper window, drew a protesting crowd that had to be dispersed by soldiers. Katherine Lysaght, nee Sexton, was also accused of having suborned her husband, Nicholas' Protestantism, by spreading Catholicism in the household and attempting to prevent his being comforted by Protestant rites on his deathbed. Failing in that, she had Nicholas' corpse dressed in a friar's habit and blessed with 'profane ceremonies.'

Arising out of the contretemps, Ald Edmund junior, the dying man's youngest son, his wife Joan, and one of his daughters, Mary Sexton, were found guilty of "high impiety and inhumanity."

Edmund and Joan were fined £5,000 and Mary £1,000 and sentenced to imprisonment for life, and all were put in the pillory for three days wearing paper hats declaring their offence. The case against Katherine Lysaght was dismissed.

Edmund at least, said Dr. Lennon, was accorded a fitting funeral, which lasted for two days and two nights, and he was interred in the family tomb in St Mary's Cathedral to rest undisturbed.

With the death of Edmund jnr, the Sexton line came to an end and succession of the vast family fortune eventually fell to Edmund Pery, an Englishman, who married Edmund's sister, Susanna, and whose son Edmund Sexton Pery was to become a prominent politician and leading developer of 18th century Limerick. His development of what was to become Newtown Pery became the hub of Limerick's burgeoning commercial and residential expansion in the late 18th century.

Ironically, in view of the contentions over the Sexton's patrimony from the 1530's onwards, it was under its awning that Catholic families such as the Arthur's, Roche's and Creagh's prospered with their own land acquisitions of developments.

Despite his failure (through premature deaths of his children and the failure of his heir to carry on the Sexton line), in his elaborate efforts to establish a family support system through ties of marriage and gossipred, Edmund, in his own opinion, maintained that his greatest achievement was to preserve the family rights to the Irish possessions of the St Mary's and Fransican Friary which he conserved for his numerous progeny.

The foregoing is an abbreviated version of Dr Lennon's fascinating lecture. The name of the Sexton family will live on particularly with the legacy of Edmund Sexton Pery, whose development of the city stands as testimony to his acumen and foresight, and whose family name is commemorated in Sexton Street, which will always be linked to CBS School, and Sexton Street North in Thomondgate, all part of the extensive lands controversially acquired by the patriarch, Edmund snr. in the far off days of the 16th century.

Halycon days in Glueyard Lane, St. Francis Abbey, circa 1950. Front: Mike Doran, Jimmy (Dutch) McNamara, Ducky (Gustine) Hayes. Centre: Peter Hayes, 'Linnet' Troy, Pa Joe Ray, Fra Hayes, Marie Wallace At back: Rose Matson, Mrs. Bridgie Frawley (nee Finnan) holding Tom (Lamb) Fitzgerald in her arms. In the background is the Clancy abode, "Dún an Oilean", built by Abbey Fisherman Jackie ("Diddles") Clancy from one of the huts used for accommodating workers in the building of the Shannon Scheme.

Bad day in Glueyard Lane

ONE Monday morning, many years ago, a character called Hadah Sweeney surveyed his cash assets and found that the bank was broken. He had been on the booze the night before and the fact that he had a great time, performing to acclaim several of his party-pieces (*Ireland Mother Ireland* was his piece de resistance) in a great sing-song in Mick Qulligan's pub, was now tempered by the fact that he had squandered the few bob set aside for that day's dinner.

He lived with fellow bachelor Mike Doran in one of the old Abbey Fishermen's cottages in Glueyard Lane in St Francis Abbey. Mike was the outstanding tenor in St. Mary's in an era when good singers were two a penny in a parish renowned for its musical acumen.

Mike sang to great acclaim in concerts and in the great pub sing-songs that abounded at that time. He was often the recipient of pints of Guinness from grateful admirers and if he had trouble finishing them, his pal Hadah would be at hand to help him out. On the departure of Mike on his marriage, Hadah became the sole incumbent of the little cottage. After protracted negotiations, which included the concessions of supplying coal and electricity, the cottage was to become the official headquarters of St. Mary's R.F.C., of which many stories have been told.

Anyway, back to the morning on which the story took place. Hadah, a builder's labourer, was more familiar with the labour exchange than the building sites, and more often than not played mammy to his more employable companion. Mike, generally ravenous after his morning's work on the building site, would be expecting his dinner at 1 o'clock, the city at that time coming to a standstill for an hour, with workers and schoolgoers coming home for the day's main meal.

Hadah, having spent the sum allotted for the meal, contemplated the larder which sadly contained just a few spuds and one head of Park cabbage.

Now while cabbage from the Park district was much sought after, flavoured as it was in gardens fertilised by the innards of pigs slaughtered in the bacon factories, cooked on its own it was quite bland.

Hadah knew that Mike would be none too pleased at such a tasteless offering. Glancing over the half door, he saw the numerous chickens that ranged freely over derelict grounds that was once the magnificent gardens of the Franciscan monks of the Abbey before Henry the VIII's cohart, Edmond Sexton, sacked and razed the priory and made off with its treasures.

Sorely tempted to lift one of the birds, the owners of which were the Rea and Mulcahy families, he knew he would be in the height of trouble if caught, as he had been accused, not without reason, of having brought to the pot some of their fowl in times past. Indeed, on one famous occasion when burning the feathers from an ill-gotten fowl, such was the purity of the white smoke that curled from the chimney that jokers in the vicinity declared that a new pope had been elected. But the owners of the lifted fowl knew better: they were a chicken less.

The odds of going undetected then, were extremely low, it being a fine summer morning with the Abbey chockfull of children playing, women at their doors knitting and gossiping, and menfolk preparing their angling cots in preparation for forthcoming regattas.

As the time for preparing the dinner approached, Hadah was now at his wit's end as he contemplated Mike Doran's face on being proffered the portly chef's choice of the day. Accepting that the option of lifting one of the chickens was now closed to him, Hadah dejectedly started to peel the few spuds when a familiar and pleasing aroma wafted through the door. It was the unmistakable smell of a pig's head being cooked and Hadah instantly knew he had been thrown a lifeline regarding the dinner.

The redolent odour was clearly coming from the house directly across the lane, known as "Dún an Oilean", built by Abbey Fisherman Jackie ("Diddles") Clancy from one of the huts used for accommodating workers in the building of the Shannon Scheme. Hadah took the few steps across to the house and after knocking, Nellie Clancy, wife of Jackie, answered the door.

"Would there be any chance" says Hadah, "you'd give me the loan of the pig's head to flavour an auld head of cabbage."

It has not been recorded if Nellie acceded to the remarkably unique request, which would have been unlikely. Neither has it been ascertained the extent of Mike Doran's language when he contemplated, after a hard morning's work on the building site, Hadah's meal of spuds and tasteless cabbage.

Tales of the Abbey Kinema

A RARE close-up of the Abbey Kinema, George's Quay, pictured shortly before it burned down in 1932. To the left is Creagh Lane, named after the distinguished Limerick family who provided many mayors and bishops to the city.

Above the houses, to the left, is the remains of the old Augustinian Chapel, built in 1778, and which according historian Lenihan was the first chapel in the city to install an organ.

The Augustinians moved to George's Street (now O'Connell Street) in 1823, where an old playhouse was converted into a church, and where in the 1940's the present substantial church was built. On the site of the houses to the left stood the Lysaght family owned Treaty Press, now Moll Darby's Restaurant.

To the right of the kinema are four storey tenements, one of which collapsed around the time of the fire, with the remainder being condemned and demolished. Families had to be accommodated in bell tents erected on the quay provided by the army. The families were re-housed in new Corporation houses in the Castle Barracks.

Broad Street's Frankie Bourke remembers attending the kinema as a youngster.

"The front seats were very cheap, but as hard as iron, but the quality improved somewhat towards the back as the prices increased.

"The kinema was owned by a Mr. Trehy and Jack Mackessy, who afterwards worked in the Lyric, was usher and ticket collector.

"These were the silent picture days and a violinist and pianist used provide the music. I heard of a film there once where Launus McNamara from St.Mary's, who had a lovely tenor voice, sang *Remona* from behind the screen in a Mexican themed film, with a Mr. Casey playing the piano."

Farranshone's Jim Cusack remembers paying a penny for admission to the kinema. "It was not that big and it was a regular thing to see people thronging the aisles and spilling on the stage, where they'd have to bend backwards to see the screen.

"There was wooden forums used in the front with everyone packed tightly together. I remember a Mr. Mackessy collecting the tickets and trying to keep us quiet, with a Mr. Casey playing the piano."

St. Anne's Technical Institute, now the School of Art, was built on the site of the kinema and tenements some years afterwards.

Views of the Past

In 1968, the Gardai were granted a five and a half day week, and Donnellan in his cartoon on the Leader, caricatured the superintendent outside William Street Barracks asking the mayor at the time, Jack Bourke, how he was going to manage.

With global warming, it is unlikely we will again see such a severe winter as that of 1963, reckoned to be the coldest of the century. Temperatures of 24 degrees f. below freezing were recorded in Limerick on the night of 24th January and the Shannon froze solid in places. Above is a group of young men standing in the middle of the swimming pool in Corbally and below, amongst those standing in the middle of the Shannon with St. Thomas' Island and St. Patrick's Church, Parteen, in the background were Maura Lysaght and Mickey (Smokey Joe) Collins at back

An unusual view of Limerick Boat Club and the Victorian dockland skyline at the turn of the 19th century, now utterly changed. Note the use that was made of the river at the time, which is dotted with yachts and pleasure rowing boats, utilised by the members of the boat club and their families in the summer, cruising upriver as far as St. Thomas' Island on the tide, complete with their picnic baskets.

Unpublished photograph of the timber boathouse (now demolished) of Athlunkard Boat Club shortly after the club was established in 1898. The present clubhouse, which was built to the left, was not erected until 1926, and the famous timber built dance hall attached to the old boathouse (since demolished) was built in the 1930's. To the left is O'Farrell's house in Athlunkard Street and on the grounds in front of the house is the club yawl, used by the members for pleasure trips upriver and down to the lower Shannon.

John and Bridie Lane outside their well stocked fruit and provision shop at 29/30 Davis Street in the years before World War II. Note the abundance of fruit such as bananas, the supply of which was to dry up as the war years progressed. In front are varied tins of Jacobs biscuits.

In this unique photograph, Mary and Carron Bedford are pictured in Keyes' Row shortly after the houses facing St. Mary's Church were demolished in the 1980's. In all, seventeen of these century old houses were demolished and replaced by just four new abodes. Many large families were reared in the old houses, the smaller residences having just two bedrooms. Some of these families included Daly/O'Connor, Gleeson, Quinlivan, Lynch, Jackson, Bourke (Athlunkard Street), Connors, Frawley, Higgins, Hayes, Whelan/Manifold, Price (Keyes' Row), Lynch, McNamara, O'Sullivan/Mullane, Hannan, Frawley, Sargent (Keeper View Terrace and Aherne's Row).

St. Mary's Choir, 1980. Back: Jimmy Clarke, Sean O'Shea, Stephen O'Shea, Christy O'Connor, Denis O'Shaughnessy, Jim Graham, Michael Yelverton, Eamonn McDonagh, Michael Hartnett, Tom Madden, Fr. John Condon, Donal Buckley, Foncie Yelverton, Joe Malone. Centre: Mary Healy, Peg Reville, Ann McCarthy, Josephine O'Connor, Marie McDonagh, Carmel O'Donoghue, Phil Healy, Geraldine O'Carroll, Mary O'Shea, Chrissie O'Brien, Jennifer O'Brien. Front: Rose Hinchey, Moira Madden, Kathleen Madden, Bridie Casey, Leonard Sheridan, conductor; Maura McNamara, Marie O'Flynn, Kitty O'Connor, Betty McNamara, Patti Houlihan

Todds, shortly before the devastating fire of 1959 which razed the whole city centre block to the ground. To the left is Patrick Street and the façade of Cruise's Hotel. A sign for Cravena cigarettes, which had been made locally in Spillane's tobacco factory, hangs over the Saxone Shoe Company. To the left of Todds is Burton's Tailors and Halpin's Grocery Store. and to the right Nicholas Tobacconists, Cromers Jewellers and Signorina Dress Shop, all destroyed in the fire. The bus on the left advertises Lambs Jam, made in Dublin. Note the sun blinds over shop windows, used to keep displayed goods from fading. The city's first traffic lights were erected at the William Street intersection shortly after this photograph was taken.

Todds fire and the Wedding Suit

TO Limerick people of a certain generation, memories of notable events concerning the city through the 1960's and 1970's still burn bright. These include the visit of John F. Kennedy to Greeenpark in 1963, Limerick's last All-Ireland senior hurling final win in Croke Park in 1973; the defeat by Munster of the invincible All Blacks in Thomond Park in 1978, and the visit of Pope John Paul II, also to Greenpark, in 1979.

Preceding these was another notable event in the city's history, that the generation of that time still have vivid memories. This was Todds department store fire which broke out on the morning of Tuesday, August 25, 1959. It was to become one of the country's and certainly the city's greatest peacetime conflagration of the 20th century, when, after spreading alarmingly to adjoining buildings, the flames threatened at one stage to raze the whole city centre to the ground.

The *Limerick Chronicle*, published in late afternoon, had 160 pt. banner headlines giving news of the fire: *Disastrous Limerick Fire. Todds and Adjoining Buildings Gutted. Many Workers Now Unemployed.* In the same issue it was announced that the contract had been signed for the building of St Munchin's College at the cost of just over a quarter of a million pounds. You could have a 15-day tour of Italy via Shannon Travel at a cost of 44 gns. and McCarthy's were selling 4 ft. solid mahogany beds at £15 10s.

On the previous Sunday, 830 passengers from the city filled two trains in the first of the famous CIE mystery train trips, which went to Cahir, Co. Tipperary. By happy coincidence the mystery train trip from Waterford also arrived in the little town and with over 1,500 roaming the streets looking for something to while the time away, it was not surprising that the pubs

As news of the fire spreads rapidly, onlookers gather in William Street

quickly ran out of beer. Many of the children from Limerick wandered around clutching buckets and shovels, the rumour being prevalent that the mystery train was bound for Tramore, which sadly proved wrong.

For well over a century, Todds (now Brown Thomas) had vied with Cannocks (now Penneys) and McBirney's (now Roche's Stores) for the title of top drapery and millinery establishment in the city.

The store was founded by William Todd in the early part of the 19th century. Apprentices in the 19th and into the 20th century lived in on the premises and fathers,

Photo taken from Roche's Stores as the fire sweeps through Todds. Staff and volunteers have salvaged all types of goods which are piled up outside the store.

mostly thriving farmers, had to pay a fee at the outset of their sons' apprenticeship. The apprentices were fully fed and found, and instead of wages, were given a small weekly allowance. Terms of indentures were very strict with visitations to ale houses and gambling dens strictly forbidden. Marriage was out of the question!

The Shannon was one of the most prolific salmon rivers in Europe at the time, and the fish being so cheap, apprentices at times were given a surfeit of the food. They objected, and had it written into their indentures that salmon would not be served more than three times a week!

Todds was synonymous with the city centre, and like Dublin's Nelson's Pillar, the rendezvous for people meeting up, especially courting couples. At the time of the fire, the store still retained its old-world Victorian

Earl Connolly (facing camera) of the Limerick Leader, was quickly on the scene. With him is Paul Goldin, hypnotist

staff feeding the cavernous stoves which heated the store.

A magnificent mahogany staircase ran from the centre of the store and at Christmastime violinist Johnny McMahon and pianist Charlie Sciascia played delightful selections of music on the stairwell, lending a wonderful yuletide atmosphere to the store. Overhead was the wholesale department, with a wrought iron balcony reminiscent of the *Titanic*, overlooking the ground floor.

Such was the trust between customer and establishment that the now long abandoned system of approbation (appro. for short) was in vogue. This was an arrangement where, if you weren't quite sure a suit, coat or dress was you, you were allowed take the item home, and fitting it on, the family or even neighbours had a gawk and gave their opinions on whether it suited you, and whether it should be retained, altered or changed.

Todds was very popular with the county tweedy types and walkers danced attendance on the more prominent of the ascendancy class, with their West Briton accents. Credit facilities were freely available, with the tried and trusted customers all having accounts there.

Joan Ryan started work in Todds shortly after the fire, but has great memories of the old premises. "The ornate stairway I remember in particular, with the red fire buckets full of sand dotted around the place. The delivery service was incredible, but it used drive us mad at times as some customers would almost expect a package of handkerchiefs to be delivered. Even the smallest items, like women's hats, would have to be wrapped and addressed for dispatch."

The magnificent moving Christmas tableaux's in the windows of Todds were always a huge attraction, and there was scarcely at child in town that did not gaze in wonder at Snow White and the Seven Dwarfs and Santa and his Reindeer. While there were imitations in other stores, it was accepted by those who still believed that the real Santa was in his grotto in the basement of

charm, with the money for your purchase being delivered overhead by wire pulley to the cashier in the office overlooking the ground floor, and your change coming back the same way.

Like Mr. Peacock in *Are You Being Served?* floor walkers in their dove-tailed frock coats, and dress striped trousers, patrolled the floors making sure that customers were being looked after, and that the impeccable reputation and standards of the emporium were being maintained.

There was a special staff of buyers who travelled the country purchasing goods at wholesale prices and also travellers, whose job it was to sell the store's merchandise to customers. There was even a full-time

Onlookers on the roof of Foley's Chemists watch the fire now completely out of control and just before the entire collapse of the building.

Todds.

For a young woman, particularly, to land a job as counter assistant in Todds was a major step up, her standing in society being greatly enhanced. It was not unknown for politicians like Ted Russell or Stevie Coughlan to put in a word with manger Andy Browne on behalf of a prospective job seeker. Ours then was a privileged family, as my sisters Maura and Theresa were

once part of this great establishment, whose annual dress dance was one of the highlights of the social calendar.

I was not long after completing my apprenticeship as a compositor in the *Limerick Leader* when on that fateful August morning news filtered through to the office that Todds was on fire. One o'clock signalled the break for dinner for schools and working places in the city, and it could not come fast enough for us to rush down and see this landmark establishment blazing.

The power and destructiveness of a fire holds morbid fascination for human beings. There is something awesome in seeing flames devouring all before them and it was not surprising that after news of the fire had spread through the city, that there were literally thousands there before us. Very little was happening in Limerick in the 1950's (an instance was that a few years previously Musical Marie brought the centre city to a standstill as she attempted to break the record for playing the piano non-stop) and the fire, then, was a huge happening with bystanders beside themselves with excitement.

We watched, frightened but enthralled, as the fire, now completely out of control, devoured all before it. Witness to the start of the fire at around 11 a.m. was messenger boy Tom Monahan from Prospect who on seeing a junction fuse box catch fire in the basement, raised the alarm. John O'Brien, secretary of the firm, rushed down with a fire extinguisher but by then the fire had got out of control and they and several staff members had to beat a hasty retreat.

Martin Ryan was working in the men's retail when the smoke started to gush up from the basement. "We tried to get to the fire but the smoke was too much and we were beaten back," he recalled.

The flames quickly spread through the building, which, over a century old, was highly inflammable. In an age when money was scarce, salvaging goods from the store became a top priority and employees and volunteers risked life and limb rescuing all sorts of merchandise before they were devoured by the flames. One of the accompanying photographs shows all sorts of salvaged commodities piled up in front of the premises. Carol (Lane) O'Toole, a young counter assistant at the time, remembers volunteers running out with the cheaper glass, and not knowing better, leaving the magnificent Waterford cut crystal behind.

The fire takes hold of the William Street section

One of the salvagers was young Dynan Fitzpatrick, who had started work in the store the year before. "We were racing out with as much glass as we could handle when part of the glass roof collapsed. We dropped everything and made a run for it," he recalled.

As news of the conflagration spread, many employees who were in a position to do so, made for the centre of the city to bear witness to the great inferno. Jim South was amongst those, managing to get away from the office in Cleeve's factory. As the fire swept towards the front of the premises, he watched in fascination as the great salvage operation reached its climax. Like many others, he decided to give a hand.

"With a Mr. O'Carroll, we were struggling to get out one of those old Victorian type cash registers when there

With the fire now out of control, hoses with pitifully small sprays of water are played futilely on the front of the building. Note the youngsters to the right in search of loot. The shades over Cannocks windows denote a sunny day.

was a mighty explosion from the back of the premises (probably a gas main erupting). We didn't hang around I can tell you," he recalled.

In a short time, the blaze had engulfed the whole premises and began to spread to adjoining establishments. The fire was exacerbated by a huge explosion when a fuel tank exploded, and periodically, massive tongues of flames shot skywards denoting the collapse of another floor.

The local fire brigade fought the flames heroically but in an era when equipment compared to now was primitive (breathing apparatus still had to come) they were practically powerless in the face of such a ferocious blaze. In all, eleven brigades fought the fire, drawn from Limerick and Cork cities, Shannon Airport, Rathkeale, Kilmallock, Charleville, Fermoy, Sarsfield Barracks, Ranks, Tipperary and Ennis.

Thirty hoses were playing on the fire at 1.30 p.m. and despite surrounding roads being closed, several cars broke through the cordon and crossing the hoses, caused them to disconnect from the hydrants. Many onlookers were drenched and fire-fighters were greatly annoyed. A

A gas main explodes in the William Street section causing intense heat and melting the paint on the Dennis fire engine.

voluntary worker, Mr. Paddy Casey, said he got drenched five times but was dry in a matter of minutes such was the intensity of the heat of the fire.

Water pressure was poor, with the outside brigades having to use hose extensions from hydrants well away from the blaze. The Shannon Airport Brigade used the hydrants near the entrance to the Prescott Burtol Cleaners, now the entrance to the Arthurs' Quay Shoppping Centre.

For the brigades, it now became a matter of containment. The dramatic collapse of the magnificent Georgian façade on to O'Connell Street was in its finality, frightening, and many of the female staff openly wept at the terrifying sight enfolding in front of them.

Charlie Daly, a member of the fire brigade, remembers the sudden collapse of the façade. "Being built of brick, it collapsed suddenly. The street was full of onlookers and it was a miracle that nobody was killed. We were hosing the front of the building when Launus McNamara, a foreman in the Corporation, and who was in the crowd, knew by the sound that the top section was about to collapse and he raised the alarm."

Adjoining premises, Lipton's grocery store, Burtons Men's Shop, and Nicholas Tobacconists and Cromer's Jewellers, were now engulfed. It looked at this stage as if the whole centre of the city would be destroyed, but valiant work by the brigades, slowly began to bear fruit. Such was the ferocity of the flames that combustion caused portion of the Garda Barracks, situated on the opposite side of William Street, to catch fire and hoses were played on it. The tyres of bikes parked at the railings started to melt.

"A gas main exploded and send a wall of heat across the road," recalled Charlie Daly. "The fire brigade tender, a 1957 Dennis, was parked nearby and nearly went up in flames. All the paint melted and eventually had to be re-sprayed."

Shops on the opposite side of O'Connell Street also had to be hosed down, with flaming debris flung like catapults across the street.

By one o'clock the situation was so serious that the Supt. J. B. O'Neill declared a state of emergency, with all streets in the vicinity being cordoned off. The military, complete with steel helmets, was called out, and under Capt. Myles Breen, did Trojan work manning hoses and keeping the streets clear.

Members of the Red Cross, Knights of Malta, St. John's Ambulance Brigade, also did invaluable work treating minor burns. The Red Cross provided a mobile canteen which served the fire brigades and volunteers, and later on the vice-chairman, Jim Hannan, thanked the Mullany sisters of Bedford Row for providing refreshments from their shop.

Another man, who offered to provide refreshments to the brigades and helpers was Pasquale Nordone of the Roma Café, who died this year. "Such was the intensity of the fire, however, that he was not allowed come down to us," recalled Charlie Daly.

The conflagration was now making international news and in a pre-television age, the local Radio Eireann correspondent, who shall be nameless, was contacted by BBC 1 Radio to give an up-to-date account of the fire. Overawed to think that the whole of England was listening in to him, the correspondent got quite excited and when asked where exactly in the city Todds was situated, he famously answered, "alongside the traffic lights!" True story.

Carol O'Toole remembers winding up sitting on the grass in the People's Park with many of the female staff. "There was no such thing as coffee shops at the time and when someone suggested we go to the park, we all followed. It was a traumatic experience, and most of the girls were in tears, wondering what would become of them."

Many school-goers headed straight for the scene instead of going back to school after dinner. Amongst them was 10-year-old Frank Healy who passing the Abbey River on his way home noticed the exceptional low state of the water and told his mother the fire

The façade collapsed suddenly just after this picture was taken.

The end. A dramatic shot as the whole building in O'Connell Street comes tumbling down. A helper in the front of the picture jumps in the air with excitement with his arms outstretched

brigades had used up all the water from the river!

Like when President Kennedy was shot, many remember where they were when they first heard of the news of the fire. Frank O'Mahony (of O'Mahony's Bookshop) was just seven years of age and was returning from Dublin by train with his father. "I have distinct memories of the headlines in the Dublin evening newspapers. I could not wait to get back to see the devastation of the fire," he recalled.

Fr. Colum Loughran O.F.M., based in central America for many years, remembers the fire quite vividly. "It coincided with the start of my novitiate in Killarney," he remembers.

Joe Malone worked in Ranks at the time and was one of six crews specially trained to deal with fires. "When news came through of the extent of the fire, the whole mill was shut down, and we were transported to the scene by lorry to fight the fire, but we did not have fire-fighting tenders," he recalled.

Another story about the fire, which we cannot vouch for, was reputed to have taken place in William Street where a section of the local Fire Brigade was in action. Many volunteers had come forward to help the brigades, and a harassed brigade member, who badly needed to make a leak, asked one of them to hold the hose while he beat a hasty retreat into a nearby laneway. The volunteer happened to be a member of the Chinese community, who would later open their first restaurant, the *Hong Kong*, further up the street. Checking around came the fire chief, and on seeing the Chinese holding the hose, said "feic me, and to think the brigade from Rathkeale hasn't arrived yet!"

As the day wore on, international news agencies began to pick up the story, which by this time had become highly embellished, with vivid descriptions of the whole city now a flaming inferno. Many emigrants, as far away as Australia and America, alarmed at the lurid accounts, anxiously rang home.

The chief of the London Fire Brigade contacted Thady McInerney, Limerick deputy chief, offering the services of his units and equipment, which would be flown into Shannon. Mr. McInerney declined the offer, saying that there was already twelve brigades fighting the fire, but was highly grateful for the offer.

Human nature being what it is, there was reports of "some acts of looting by an incorrigible section of the community but on a small scale" according to the

After the front façade collapsed.

Leader, which went on to say that "the response to appeals for assistance and help to remove salvaged goods was met with a response that was a grand reflection of the really true Christian spirit that exists in Limerick."

Some of those salvaged goods were reputed to have surfaced later on in the day with certain customers in surrounding pubs splendidly arrayed in span new sports coats!

There was another popular yarn about a character from Janesboro, who seizing his chance when he saw an unopened parcel in Todds Bow, rushed home with it thinking he'd have material for a suit. When he opened it up, to his horror, it contained brown shrouds, or habits as we used call them.

Another soul, spotting some unattended suit lengths, helped himself. His conscience later came at him and he went to confession in the Franciscans, the priest warning him "not make a habit out of it!"

One of the extraordinary things about the conflagration was that there was no one killed or even badly burned, minor abrasions being the only injuries reported. A miracle indeed, considering the intensity of the fire, and the close proximity of the crowds.

One of those who had a narrow escape was a deaf mute, working in the tailoring department. He was in the toilet cubicle when the fire took hold and could not hear the racket outside. One of his workmates, realising the situation, pushed papers under the door to attract his attention, and he got out safely.

Buyer Paddy Fitzpatrick, who was on holidays with his wife Byrdie in the Isle of Man, had his vacation interrupted when son Dynan telephoned him to inform him of the catastrophe.

The Mayor, Ald. John Carew, was also on holidays, in Kilkee, and he received a telegram from Ald. Steve Coughlan requesting him to return and call a special meeting of representatives of prominent city groups in view of the great hardships caused, and to take some

A happier occasion: following the fire, the management of Todds organised a dinner dance as a thank you to the staff for their co-operation during and after the fire. Enjoying the function were staff members Mary Ryan and Paddy O'Dwyer.

steps to alleviate the distress of the employees affected. The Mayor complied, and there was an immediate response to an appeal.

Limerick Boat Club announced that the entire proceeds of their dance on Sunday night at the Stella would be handed over to the fund. Keane's Bakery, Parnell, Street, handed in a cheque of £100 to the *Leader*, and a similar one was received from Danus clothing factory. Within a few days, £1,000 had been collected, with a promise of more.

Notwithstanding the success of the appeal, the writer of Current Review in the *Chronicle*, was in pessimistic mood. "When a similar disaster occurred to Roche's Stores eleven years ago, hundreds became unemployed, and many had to seek work elsewhere. Now the same fate awaits the unfortunate employees of Messrs. Todds and the result may mean the breaking up of many homes."

Many others were affected by the fire, particularly those living in the vicinity. Christy Doran, artist, whose studio was over Burtons, lost all his possessions. Hairdresser Harry O'Sullivan, who had his salon over Nicholas', also lost all his equipment, as did Mr; Ferris, of Cesar's hairdressers.

With many of the burnt out buildings now in a dangerous state, it was found necessary to keep the main thoroughfares closed in the days following the fire. City centre business came to a standstill, which prompted the Mayor and the president of the Chamber of Commerce to call on the Garda Superintendent to express their concern.

There was bad news for those who thought their accounts with Todds went up in smoke with the fire. The one and half ton safe, which crashed into the basement, was rescued and when opened by an expert locksmith from Dublin, £500 in cash was intact and more importantly, all the firm's ledgers and accounts. Two mementos of sentimental value were also rescued: two covers of packing cases, one showing the legend "by steam to Dublin, hence by canal to Todds," and the other dated 1836.

The show wasn't over yet. It was announced by the demolishers, Sheehy Bros., from Kilcornan, that a helicopter with the aid of ball and chain would be used in the demolition of the burn out buildings and on September 12th, thousands of onlookers turned up to make their first sight of this wondrous machine. The helicopter was transported from Hampshire in a Dakota aircraft and reassembled in Shannon.

Meanwhile, it was back to work within a short time for the employees of the firm with the carpet section on

The aftermath: With the dangerous state of the remaining walls, it was decided to use a helicopter to demolish these with the aid of a ball and chain. For the vast majority of Limerick people, it was their first sight of a helicopter and they turned out in their thousands to see the demolition. In the background can be seen William Street Garda Barracks and Imco Cleaners.

the opposite side of William Street being utilised, and temporary premises acquired in Spillane's Tobacco Factory in Sarsfield Street Bargain hunters scored heavily: several sales followed on, with most of the salvaged stock being in good condition.

A young local man, Stuart Klien bargained with manager Andy Browne for the salvaged lead which had lined the roofs of the store. He did well, and maintained

the profit he made set him on his way on his business career.

There was one extraordinary story about the salvaged goods. Let Martin Ryan tell it to us: "A Feakle woman had purchased her wedding suit but unfortunately it was still in the store undergoing alterations at the time of the fire. She was quite upset and insisted she wanted that particular suit even though

The end: Photograph, taken from Thomas Street, shows the extent of the fire with the whole block having been razed to the ground. Roches Stores, Cannocks, the Saxone and William Street Barracks can be seen in the background with Sheehy Bros. (demolishers) crane to the right.

manager Andy Browne kept explaining that it went up with the fire. We were sorting the salvaged goods in the Belltable and Andy, describing the suit, said to me to keep an eye out for it, by some miracle it might have survived. I was flabbergasted when not alone did I come across the suit, but it was in perfect condition."

The Saturday previous to the fire, staff member Joan Reddan left to get married. Luckily, she took her wedding dress with her, which was made specially in Todds under the supervision of seamstress Miss McMahon. A reporter in the *Irish Independent* got wind that the dress had gone up in the fire and Joan, to her astonishment, read headlines in the Indo to the effect that her wedding dress had gone up in flames. "I couldn't believe the crowd that turned up for the wedding. I'm sure they half expected to see me getting

Todds dress dance was one of the city's social events of the season. The committee, pictured just six months before the fire, was (front row): Dynan Fitzpatrick, Mr. and Mrs. Mick Murphy, Statia Grennan and Brian Fitzgerald. Centre: Michael Twomey, Sean O'Brien, Sean Hanrahan, Martin Griffin. Back row: Martin Ryan, Eddie Duignan, Martin Smalle, Paddy Fitzpatrick

Attending the dress dance were Back: Tom Nix, Sean Hanrahan ----- Bobs Walsh, Paddy O'Toole, Sean O'Brien. Front: ------ Mrs. Browne, Andy Browne, Carol Lane, Mrs. O'Brien.

At a function to wish Nuala O'Connor (centre) bon voyage on her new job in Shannon Duty Free in the late 1950's were her workmates in Todds: Back: Statia Grennan, M. O'Connor, Phyllis Hickey, Mary Meehan, Bridie Hannigan, Joan Clohessy. Centre: Helen Kennedy, Mary Geary, Joan Reddan, Nuala O'Connor, Joan Holland, Breda Tracey, M Kelly. Front: Paggy Murphy, -------, Rita O'Shea, Theresa O'Shaughnessy, Ita Colbert, Carole Lane, Bridie O'Brien.

married in rags or something," Joan recalled.

Members of the staff, who worked all hours sorting goods after the fire, did not receive any extra payment, a criterion of the times that were in it. The directors, as a thank you, organised a dinner dance in Cruise's Hotel for all the staff, which despite the trauma of the fire, was enjoyed by all.

One man who had painful memories of the demolition of the gutted buildings was the late Mick Gleeson, proprietor of P. J. Gleeson licensed premises at the corner of Todds Lane at 68 William Street. Michael Gleeson, of Gleeson Shoes, William Street, a nephew of the proprietor, takes up the story:

"The idea behind the use of the helicopter was to knock the walls inwards with ball and chain, maximising damage to adjoining buildings.

Unfortunately, when a wall near the pub was knocked it fell the wrong way and caused structural damage. There was a huge wrangle about the insurance, the companies involved claiming it was each other's responsibility. It went to law, and after dragging on for five years, my uncle eventually sold the pub for £10,000." Not a great price even for that time, for a city centre pub.

A sad conclusion to the fire was the sudden death of the owner of Todds, Mr. Buckley, the day after the fire. His death was the only casualty, indirectly, of the inferno. "We were at his funeral in Fermoy within a day or two of the fire. It was generally accepted that the shock of the fire had a traumatic effect on him," recalled Martin Ryan.

Todds was rebuilt and the new premises was opened on May 31, 1963, with Mass being celebrated on the main floor by Monsignor Moloney. In a letter written the week before, manager Andy Browne made an appeal to the staff: "Between now and opening day, a great deal of work has to be done, but the management feel confident that they will receive the same wholehearted co-operation from the staff as they had received in the past. Between now and opening day, there may be times when our endeavours will be stretched to the limit, but I feel that with co-operation and good humour, any difficulties arising will be easily overcome."

Todds was back and flourishing again, but sadly the glass and plastic architectural era had dawned, and the new building was a long way off the old premises. The magnificent stonework of the Georgian façades, both in O'Connell and William Street, are now only recalled from faded photographs.

The store was taken over in 1964 by Switzers of Dublin and in 1971 Waterford Glass, in an amalgamation with Harrods, took over the Switzer Group on a 60/40 basis. Browne Thomas, the present proprietors, took over later on. Andy Browne, general manager, who will always be associated with Todds, retired in 1970.

The amount of people employed by Todds around the time of the fire, in an age before self-service did away with a lot of jobs, can be gauged from the following list, drawn up by some of the staff members who worked there at the time (there will be omissions as memories become dimmed after almost fifty years!): Andy. Browne, general manager; Sean O'Brien, Mick Twomey, Donal Moloney, George Creaney, Cecil Smith, M. Gailbraith, Martin Ryan, M. J. Lynch, Randall Counihan, Bob Walsh, T. Clarke, Martin. Griffin, R. Kelly, Joe McNamara, Reenie Glasgow, John Daly, Sean. Hanrahan, Tom Ryan, Jim Beary, Willie. Sheehan, Paddy O'Connor, Tom Harrington, Willie Harrington, Martin Smalle, Vincent. O'Connor, Dynan. Fitzpatrick, Johnny Markham, Tom Liddane, Tom O'Connor, Nessan Johnson, Ml. Haran, Sean Foley.

Willie Hough, Ml. Cunneen, Paddy Maher, M. Kelly, Johnny Merner, N. Fitzgerald, Haulie Dargan, Louise Cremin, Hugh. O'Donovan, Joe McNamara, Ml. McInerney, jnr.; L. Hickey, J. Morrissey, Paddy Nevin, Ml. McInerney snr.; L. Naughton, Maurice McAuliffe, Eddie Duignan, Kieran Slattery, Maurice. Ryan, Jack Molyneaux, Tony McCormack.

Buyers: M. Russell, Ml. McMahon, Ml. Neville, Tom McInerney, Ned Franklin, Paddy Fitzpatrick, Eugene McGovern, Tom O'Grady, Dan Reddan, Dan Fitzgibbon, M. Burke, Miss Haslam.

Travellers: Jim Cleary, Sean. Cleary jnr.; Paddy O'Dwyer, Jim Griffin, Tom Nix, Brian Fitzgerald.

Office: Susan Dillon, Bridie Kennedy, Betty McMahon, Biddy Griffin, Finola Murphy, Mary Meade, Marie Lane, A. Tuohy,

Carpeting, upholstery: Paul Bernard, Larry Devaney, Jack O'Shea, Andy Murphy, Malachy Hanley, Michael Molyneaux, Willie Ronan, Bill McGuire, Conor McGuire, Michael Slattery.

Tailoring: Mick Murphy, Josie Quinlivan, Johnny Donovan, Jack Lawlor.

Office boys: Charlie. McLean, Tom Nix Jnr., A. Mulvihill.

Women employees in the various departments were: Ursula Grady, Mary Geary, Margaret Spearin, Carol Lane, Joan Ashling, Joan Cleare, Mary McDonagh, Miss Noonan, Rita O'Shea, Theresa O'Shaughnessy, Nellie Greaney, Statia Grannel, Mary Moloney, Ita O'Donovan, Joan Holland, Mary Greaney, Mary McMahon, Mary McCormack, Mary O'Brien, Judie Gilligan, Jean Fitzpatrick, Joan Reddan, Teresa O'Neill, Mai O'Dwyer, G. O'Grady, Miss Haslem, Miss Houlihan, B.O'Brien, Patricia O'Kelly, Kitty O'Dwyer, Ethel O'Connor, Miss Brouder, Nancy Cosgrove, Kathleen Ryan, Teresa Clancy, M. McInerney, Peggy Devereaux, C. Menighan, Mary Ryan, Mary O'Connor.

All smiles in Todd's new premises 1960's

108

St. John's Christian Brothers' School

Scabby Lane and a strike in St John's

DICK Naughton, the late venerable *Limerick Chronicle* journalist, has recorded some of the laneways and alleys that spine-like ran from Broad Street and John Street in former times. Practically all of these have disappeared including Scabby Lane, a name which was recalled when a visiting American called to the Chronicle, inquiring to know if his parents could really have been born in such an inelegantly named place. No-one back in the States would believe him that anyone could name a lane thus, but Dick, having an old St John's school register in his possession, was able to tell him that indeed such a place existed, located off Broad Street.

Many of these lanes had quaint appellations, examples being Magdalen Lane, Repeal Alley, Flag Lane, Pencil's Lane, Forker's Lane, Gallow's Green, Joshue's Lane, Clampett's Bow, Mass Lane, Hatters Lane, etc.

Many of the lanes were named after personalities: thus you had Fr. Quin Lane, with Sheehy, Smith, Moloney, Williams, Monaghan, Barrett, Hogg, Carey, Brennan, all having their names perpetuated by having lanes and rows named after them.

The school registry mentioned was that of St John's CBS of the 1850's and a list of the pupils showed some of the quaint occupations their fathers had, which included rag pickers, scavengers, snuff makers, ragmen, cagemakers, salters, stagekeepers, whip and basket makers, wool-card makers, brickmakers, varnishers, tinkers, gravediggers, coffin makers, etc.

Just a few years after the Great Famine, the object poverty then abounding intruded into the registry with comments such as "at home, very poor", "gone to workhouse", "at home, minding his mother", "parents dead, ran away" and the name of an eleven year old boy was struck off as "he had left to go to work."

Most poignant entry was that concerning John Holihan of Garryowen, aged 7 years, whose date of leaving school was September 7, 1859. And the reason was simply marked "buried today."

One of the most remarkable incidents in the history of the school, or indeed of any school in the city, took place in the late 1930's when pupils of fifth and sixth classes staged a strike, a happening unprecedented in the city in those times.

Seemingly the boys of St John's, when they assembled after the fist day of the summer holidays, became incensed when they heard that the boys in Sexton Street had received an additional day's holiday and were not required to return to school until the following day. The senior boys conferred, and decided that they too, would have their day off even if it meant absconding.

Confining the dispute to the two senior classes, the boys vacated the school en masse and hit for Plassey to spend the day as they thought gambolling in the surroundings of the verdant countryside.

They had not reckoned with their principal, however, a well built Corkman named Bro. O'Regan, who quaintly passed the school breaks away by strolling around the yard on a pair of stilts! Like many of the Brothers he had a nick-name, and was called King Kong after the highly popular film of the time showing at the Lyric.

Bro. O'Regan, on hearing of the destination of the truants, sped off in hasty pursuit and caught up with the culprits as they approached the Groody River. Knowing the fate that lay in store for them, the errant schoolboys jumped across the narrow confines of the river. Bro. Regan did likewise, but not being as supple as the young strikers, he landed in the middle of the stream, and the boys made good their escape. You could say that they were really in hot water now. Their escape was only a temporary reprieve.

Next day recriminations and reprisals took place with summary justice being meted out via the Brothers' infamous leather strap. One of the ring-leaders was the late Matthew Sheedy, and he was signalled out for special treatment. His inquisitor was one of the local priests from St John's, who had been sent for such was the seriousness of the breach of discipline. As an example to the assembled pupils, he drew out on Matthew with all his might, hitting him on the side of the head. Matthew's ear-drum was perforated in the blow, and he lost his hearing in that ear as a result. It would have been unheard of to sue a man of the cloth at that time and his parents didn't even think of making a claim.

Matthew, however, coped with the handicap and he went on to become one of the city's best loved and most accomplished entertainers, singer and accordionist, for a period that lasted half a century and more.

Johnny O'Driscoll Band, 1940's. From left: Matthew Sheehy, Michael Danford, John O'Driscoll, Jim Owen, Felix Lynch.

Reflections on Corbally

A MAGNIFICENT aerial view of St. Munchin's College, Corbally, (left) taken by Donal McMonagle of the *Leader* during the course of construction, 1960. A substantial mansion known to generations as the Bishop's Palace was demolished to make way for the new college. The residence (formerly named *Corbally*) dated back to the early 19th century and was built by Pierce Shannon, an entrepreneur of the time, who bought the surrounding lands from the Monsell family, and on which the substantial houses on the Mill Road were built.

Shannon had more luck than successive Limerick Corporations regarding extension of the city boundary. At the time, the whole district of Corbally and Park was in Co. Clare, and Shannon used his influence as Mayor to have these areas brought inside the city boundary. He did it just in time: he dropped dead conducting a meeting of the Corporation shortly afterwards, in 1844.

The sites of several historical events can be seen in this splendid photograph.

On the right hand shore of the river were what was traditionally known as the Church Fields (now Shannon Banks housing estate) where on fine summer Sundays generations of families walked with laden prams from the city to picnic and disport themselves in the unpolluted Shannon.

Further down the Church Fields the Williamite forces forded the river in the Siege of Limerick, 1691. At this spot stood a large rock which was called Carraig-a-Clouragh, in Gaelic, which in English means the chain rock. It was here that the Williamite engineers built a pontoon bridge, the chains of which were attached to this rock, which enabled the English army to make the crossing.

The top of the rock was pock-marked with little holes and sometimes at certain times after rain the water in the indentions turned a reddish colour. The legend was that the water was actually blood, symbolic of the treacherous act of betrayal*. Visitors to the city, including men of science, archaeologists, historians, and huge crowds came out from town, to view it according to historian Lenihan.

In later years, the owner of the lands, Captain Hamilton Jackson, ordered a servant named Connell to blow up the rock to deter crowds from trespassing on the lands. The poor worker was badly injured when the explosive went off prematurely and this of course added to the legend, most of the rock surviving the blast. The remains of the rock were swallowed up by the expansion of the river when the Shannon Scheme was built.

The Red Path, built by the Corporation in the 1940's, runs along the left foreshore and a sharp angle opposite the college tells the story of an aborted attempt to build a bridge across the Shannon in early 19th century. This was before the present Athlunkard Bridge was built in 1830 (in forefront of picture). A banker, James Kennedy, conceived the idea and for a start laid the foundations for an approach road with a substantial clearance through a small hill, the indention of which can still be seen in the grounds of the college. The next stage was the building of an abutment or arch (still extant) but after this the project failed, the late Kevin Hannan maintaining that the might of the river asserted itself and the scheme was abandoned. The older generation called this abutment Kennedy Bridge.

Further down the path can be seen the shelters and changing area (now demolished) of the swimming pool, the fields behind it now containing substantial housing estates. Across from the pool can be seen the damming wall in the middle of the river, built to form the Mill Stream whose waters turned the wheels of Corbally Mills, sited where the path begins.

To the right of the wall is St. Thomas' Island, where in the 13th century the Dominicans built a monastery, not a stone of which is extant. The boundary walls and the remains of a substantial house can be seen in the middle of the island. The Tuthill's were the best known of several families who lived there and a one-time resident is reputed to have been confined to the island for six days of the week, being unable to cross to the mainland only on Sundays, when he was immune from the attentions of a process server (writs being prohibited from being served on Sundays). At the end of the island can be seen the remains of the historic Lax Weir, reputedly built by the Vikings, and further on, to the right, the opening into the Tail Race.

*A fisherman by the name of Philip McAdam, is reputed to have revealed the river crossing to the Williamites. He is buried in Kilquane graveyard (the area top right of the picture, but not visible in picture) and his grave for generations was heaped with many indignities by people visiting the graveyard, including bodily functions.

A couplet was carved on his tombstone, "here lies the body of Philip the traitor, lived a fisherman and died a deceiver" but was removed by his family, only to have it carved again repeatedly. His descendants hotly denied McAdam's alleged act of treachery, and told Lenihan this in no certain terms when he was compiling his history.

Three Germans, Heir Firestone, Josef Hainer and Rudolph Weigal, killed accidentally during the building of the nearby Shannon Scheme, are also buried there, as is Fr. Matthew Moloney, parish priest of St. Mary's during the Siege of Limerick, 1690-91. He was the last priest to celebrate Mass in St. Mary's Cathedral.

Corbally swimming pool was in the height of its popularity around the time of the building of the nearby St. Munchin's College With the completion of the Main Sewerage Scheme, and a return to promised pristine waters, it is hoped that the swimming pool may be renewed.

Mayor Jim Casey performing the opening ceremony of the Savoy, December 19th, 1935.

When *God Save the Queen* was played in the Savoy

PICTURE the scene. It is Sunday night in the late 1950's, the most popular drinking night of the week in an era of early closing hours. Sounds of great sing-songs emanate from pubs in Broad Street, particularly Mick Quilligan's, where in the front of the house (known as the officers' quarters) aficionados from musical St. Mary's families make dissertations on the qualities of the various performers. Sunday night is not the traditional musical night in Quilligan's, but exceptions are being made in deference to some returned Yanks.

There is an hour to go to closing time and the singers are in full flow. Suddenly, the musical accord is shattered by the sound of a bunch of keys being scraped and banged against the frosted glass door panel leading on to Lough Quay. It is the proprietor's ear-shattering warning to patrons to disperse and seek another hostelry to display their musical acumen.

And for what reason on this, the most lucrative night of the week for takings, should a publican throw out his customers an hour before their allotted time?

It was the Savoy you see. Confirmed bachelor Mick Qulligan had his ticket booked for the Sunday night performances in the Bedford Row cinema and even if it meant throwing his customers prematurely into the cold night, so be it.

Such was the allure of the Savoy.

On holidays in Salthill in the late 1950's, one of our group revved up his motor bike early one Sunday might. "Where are you off to?" we enquired. "Oh, I forgot I had tickets booked for the Savoy for myself and the girl-friend". And off he sped, to return at all hours of the morning to our guest house, Loyola, in Salthill.

Another man who rarely missed a Sunday night performance was Jacko Moynihan, the legendary shoemaker from Mungret Street, whose famous bus excursions gave struggling working class people the chance to visit Kilkee or Ballybunion at least once a year.

Jacko booked early in the week, and proudly displayed his ticket on a nail in the shop. A declaration to all and sundry where he would be that Sunday night.

What was the allure of the Savoy that would make a publican miss out on some serious takings, a cobbler display his ticket like a prize trophy, a young man interrupt his holidays to be part of the audience that invariably filled the vast cinema on Sundays and most nights of the week?

The Savoy had class. Simple as that. For a city that was accustomed to draughty, flea-infested halls posing as cinemas (the Tivoli in Charlotte Quay was called the Bug House) and with hard benches and unmentionable sanitary arrangements, the new venue was the last word in luxury, with its gleaming foyer, restaurant and bar. The ambiance was Moorish inspired, lavish tapestries on the walls and surrounding the stage, moulded imitation balconies, and myriad little lights reflecting from the ceiling and walls to denote the sparkling stars of an Arabian night.

What bliss. It was a step into the Orient. The nearest patrons of the Thomond got to seeing imitations of stars was when bla'guards flicked their lighted cigarette butt ends from the balcony into the crowd seated on the wooden benches below them!

Then there was the Compton organ, rising like a brightly illuminated submarine from the depths of the pit, exuding an infinite variety of delicate and colourful tones we had never heard before. The organist was its commander, saluting the patrons as his instrument rose still higher, filling the front of the stage in a kaleidoscope of sound and colour. In a pre-television age, we sang our hearts out, with songs of the words appearing on screen well before karaoke was copied from the Japanese. Gordon Spicer, Fred Bridgeman, Jack Courtney, Norman Metcalfe, Stanley Bowyer (Brendan and Olive O'Brien's father) and our own John Enright were the accomplished organists that entertained us.

The tip-up seats were an innovation also, and the odd patron, using them for the first time, initially sat on them while they were tipped back! Lynwood Park's Paddy Power remembered his father taking them to the Savoy in the early years, and he had to tell his dad to tip forward the seat as initially he sat down on the edge! Many will remember the huge safety curtain plastered with advertisements. It weighed four tons, and had to be tested on a daily basis

If you met someone at a dance, a date for the Savoy was a splendid beginning to a possible relationship. All the better still if you had tickets for the balcony on Sunday night, and if you produced a box of Black Magic, you were home and dried. The opulent cinema played its part in helping cement budding courtships, and many couples of long wedded bliss will surely testify to this.

The Savoy was opened amidst great fanfare on 19th December, 1935, by the Mayor, M. J. Casey. *City's Night of Triumph*, trumpeted the *Leader* the following day. Proprietors were Irish Cinemas Ltd. who built the same complexes in Cork and Dublin, and also owned the Theatre Royal.

Foundations had been laid in Bedford Row in January, 1935, on the site of a derelict grain store, and the cinema was opened eleven months later. There was a big emphasis on employing local labour and Limerick

The magnificent interior of the Savoy, pictured by Michael Cowhey before its demolition.

firms such as McMahon's and Spaight's supplied much of the building material. Manager was Jack Sheil, who was recruited from Cleeve's toffee and condensed milk factory. Alan Chambers from the Theatre Royal gave what the *Leader* described as a delightful recital on the Compton organ. A first-class restaurant was also opened in plush surroundings. The building cost of the complex was put at between £30,000 and £40,000.

The 1930's was an era of great unemployment and the building of the Savoy was a great boost to local construction workers with three hundred being employed in its building. One of the stone masons employed was Michael Kemmy, who due to financial constraints, could not afford to marry his sweetheart, Elizabeth Pilkington. Neither was he in a position to emigrate, as many of his fellow workers had done. But with gainful employment at last, the couple were in a position to get married. So, who knows, but only for the construction of the Savoy we might never have known Jim Kemmy!

The first film shown was *Brewster's Millions* starring Jack Buchanan. Admission prices were 7d, 1/3, and 2/- (balcony). There was no Sunday performances as films were not allowed to be shown in Limerick on the Sabbath on the instructions of the bishop. It was the golden age of the cinema and the following week Fredric March and Charles Laughton starred in *Les Miserables* followed by Jeanette McDonald and Nelson Eddy in *Naughty Marietta*.

From the outset, a very strict sense of staff discipline and dress code was introduced and to implement this, the imposing commissionaire from Dublin's Savoy, John Ferris, was brought down to implement it. He stood at 6' 3'', and weighed seventeen stone with a chest measurement of 50 inches. There would have been very little back-answering from the staff.

The first two page boys employed were Gussie Malone and Michael Horrigan at the princely sum of 12s. 6d. per week.

The dress code was continued down the years, and former manager Tom English recalls the inspection which took place in early afternoon before the first showings. "It was like Willie O'Dea inspecting an army guard of honour, with stage manager Alec O'Farrell walking down the line critically analysing the uniforms of usherettes and page boys."

Films were not the only form of entertainment and music lovers were absolutely spoiled when in the space of a month, shortly after the opening, three of the world's greatest artistes performed in the 1,500 seater cinema/theatre. These included such legends as the American basso, Paul Robeson, our own tenor John McCormack, and Fritz Kreisler, the famous violinist. They were brought here by Harold Holt, described as the world's greatest musical impressario.

Patrons could hear any of the foregoing legends in the Savoy for the admission price of three shillings, equivalent to 19 cents in Euro today! Many patrons paid 150 Euros to hear Pavarotti sing in the Point Theatre last year.

Robeson, described in the Leader as a "negro vocalist" stayed in Cruise's Hotel and when he took a stroll through the city, it was reported that the natives, unused to seeing blacks, stopped in their tracks when he passed, with some even following him. When asked the inevitable question, "what did he think of Limerick," Robeson replied, "the people are very friendly but oh, they are so curious!"

In the course of the recital, Robeson sang the song that he had made famous, *Ole Man River* from *Showboat*, and many negro spirituals such as *Swing Low Sweet Chariot* and *Joshua Fit de Battle ob Jericho*. He was described as having a wonderful personality and with his magnificent physique had a commanding stage presence. He was required to give four encores which

Michael Ryan, commissionaire, and Nancy Kirby (nee Burke), usherette, outside the Savoy foyer in the 1950's.

included *My Old Kentucky Home.*

Mr. Robeson, at the conclusion of the concert, was wildly applauded and giving thanks, he said he was very grateful to the citizens of Limerick for the cordiality of their reception. "This was my first visit to Limerick but I hope to come back again and again (applause). I have many friends in America from Limerick, and I will write to tell them of the great time I have had in their home town." (applause).

Within two weeks of Robeson's performance, on February 18th, 1936, our own John McCormack was given an ecstatic reception. Comments overheard after the concert included "there's no one to beat him" and "there's only one McCormack." So many tried to gain admission that a large amount of extra seating was placed at the back of the stage, and in acknowledgment McCormack turned round and faced them when singing *The Rose of Tralee.*

"What most struck those present who had heard McCormack when he was in the height of his power and fame is the remarkable degree to which he has retained his marvellous voice. A quarter of a century had rolled by since our matchless Irish tenor first brought the world to its feet, at a time when Caruso was earning £500 a night in New York. Today he has as much sweetness as ever while his unequalled artistry is absolutely unimpaired' reported the *Leader*. "His singing of 'Little Boy Blue' was marked with a delightful sweetness but put into it an amount of feeling and tender pathos calculated to send the most unemotional into something of a melting mood."

Interestingly, McCormack had five years previously captivated a capacity audience in St John's Pavilion, a venue where the famous Australian baritone, Peter Dawson, performed a few years later. There is a conception that Gigli, the famous tenor, also sang in the Savoy and St John's, but this is not correct. Local newsboy, the late Fonsie Reidy, was a great fan of the Italian singer, and was invited personally to hear him sing in Covent Garden, where afterwards he was introduced backstage.

The last, but by no means least, of this world famous trio to perform at the Savoy in the opening weeks was the legendary Austrian, Fritz Kreisler, who captivated the house with his virtuoso violin playing. In the run-up to the concert, music lovers were exhorted: "until you have heard Kreisler play, you have no idea as to the great heights that music can reach. It is the duty of everyone to hear this great world master who holds the whole world in subjection to the beauty of his art."

While the concert was booked out, there were several vacant seats, owing to the death of King George V. It is likely that these cancellations would have come from the last vestiges of the ascendancy class in the county. The *Leader* had some reservations about Kreisler's programme, mentioning that no doubt that it was in the main severely classical and above the heads of many of the audience.

The shadow of Hitler was now looming large in Europe and despite travel restrictions during the war, many of the world's greatest artistes, including the legendary Australian soprano Joan Hammond, made it to the Savoy. Some of the great opera companies, including the Carl Rosa, and the Dublin Grand Opera Company, entertained during the war years.

Hailed as the new John McCormack, Askeaton-born tenor Christopher Lynch packed out the Savoy every time he performed in the 1940's. His career came to a sudden and mysterious end when he was at the height of his popularity both here and America. It was said that he just got fed up of the life and packed in.

McCormack had trained the Askeaton singer and stated that he was his natural successor.

Another popular visitor was Jack Doyle, "The Gorgeous Gael." The Cobh-man, boxer/entertainer, was married to the movie star Movita (who later married Marlon Brando) and their relationship was at the best of times tempestuous. Part of a husband and wife act, Movita failed to appear one night, the announcement being that she was indisposed. The indisposition included a black eye, administered by the Gorgeous Gael!

The late forties and early fifties was the great era of the "cine-variety", with its mixture of live entertainment and films. With the theatre in England in disarray after the war, many well-known British and European artistes appeared in the Savoy. They were not overly paid but were glad of the work and good food which was still very scarce in England and the continent due to

May Bermingham, long-serving and highly popular member of the staff of the restaurant.

rationing.

The virtuoso violinist, Yehudi Menuhin, was one of the world famous stars to play in the Savoy and anxious to meet him was local band leader and violinist Johnny McMahon, who had a very old violin, the worth of which he wanted Yehudi to assess. Tom English arranged the meeting and the two violinists were snapped for the *Leader*. "Who's that fella with Johnny?" local wags wanted to know.

Limerick artistes, too, were making their mark at the Sunday night concerts. These included Michael McNamara, James Penny, Hilda Roche, Michael McCann snr., etc. Amongst them was a young soprano named Josephine Scanlon, who was to go on to become a household name in opera.

The fact that there was a live show with the films, meant there was no tax, which made these shows popular with proprietors. The Savoy complexes by this time were taken over by Odeon Theatres, run by the English Rank family, well established in Limerick already as millers on the Dock Road. The Ranks were of course film makers themselves, but looking back on them, most of the J. Arthur Rank productions were very forgettable.

In the late 1940's, a young lad named Joe Malone from St. Mary's joined the staff. He had graduated from grocery shop messenger boy to the lofty position of page-boy (or Buttons as they were sometimes called). Complete with pill-box hat, white gloves, striped pants and black patent shoes, he was the envy of his former messenger boy compatriots as he strutted up O'Connell Street on errands. He proudly overheard a woman one day saying "isn't he the real Ally Daly!"

The President of Ireland, Sean T. O'Ceallaigh, one year officially opened the Feile Luimni in the Savoy. Joe gleamed, and like the rest of the staff was drilled in protocol for the great occasion. In his excitement, Joe walked too far ahead of the President and wound up leading the procession alongside Bean Ui Ceallaigh, the President's wife, who stood at least a head over the Sean T. Joe got a smart tap on the head from an aide to make way for the president to walk beside his wife.

Next day Joe was in the bookie office when he heard a woman who was looking at the *Cork Examiner* saying to a companion, "isn't the president a dotey little fella." Looking over her shoulder, Joe saw a photograph of himself alongside Mrs. O'Ceallaigh with his pill-box to one side and the President walking behind the two of them!

One of the most popular entertainers to have played the Savoy was Eamonn Andrews who compered the quiz show *Double Or Nothing* in the early 1950's. All you needed was to step from the audience on to the stage and there you were in front of 1,500 people endeavouring to answer general knowledge questions put by the charmer from Dublin, who was later to go on to become a household name in television.

Many a struggling housewife supplemented meagre housekeeping money by coming out as winners (as a youngster, I watched apprehensively as my own mother won a couple of quid). The trick was not to push your luck, quit while ahead before the questions became too difficult because you lost all if you missed a question. Eamonn often helped by giving timely prompts to those who were struggling.

Better known at the time as a radio boxing commentator, Eamonn compered the Imco Cleaners sponsored show live on Radio Eireann in Dublin at lunch-time on Thursdays. He had to be back at the Savoy by 5.30 for the first performance of the quiz and with dual carriageways a thing of the future, it was a tight schedule.

Not a renowned driver himself, Eamonn used the services of several drivers until stuck one day, he took the wheel of the car himself. With him was stage manager, Alec Farrell, going to see Dublin for the first time. Rushing from the Metropolis, Eamonn took the bend entering Monastaraven too sharply, and in straightening out the car, the driver's door became unhinged and the future compere of *This is Your Life*, in tandemn with Alec Farrell, found themselves cast on to the road. The now driverless car careered on to the frontage of a local Garda's house, taking the drainpipe with it. It took thirty shillings to placate the irate Garda for the loss of his drainpipe.

There were further repercussions. Driving the doorless car on to Limerick, Eamonn discovered his introduction to the hard surface of the road had taken the seat of his trousers away!

With the show now well behind schedule (the organist had played the Double or Nothing introduction several times), the audience was getting restless. Joe Malone, who from repetition was very familiar with the show, was about to take over when the bold Eamonn arrived, breathless and dishevelled. And to a mystified audience, the suave, charming Dubliner compered the show attired in his Cromby overcoat, for a reason that was known only to himself and Alec.

Two local characters, the late Poet Ryan and Major Roche-Kelly, a First World War veteran who lived as a recluse in Cappanty, practically made a living from the quiz. Anyone could come up from the audience and both often appeared at the matinee and evening performances. Eventually, Eamonn, over a couple of drinks, told them their *Double or Nothing* career was terminated!

Unbelievably, no films were allowed to be shown in Limerick on Sundays by order of the bishop until circa 1950, the only place in the country to have such a ban. There was no films allowed either during Holy Week. During this archaic prohibition, especially during the war years, Muintir na Tire, under its founder Fr. Hayes, organised concerts on the Sunday nights which quaintly had discussions on matters of national importance plus musical entertainment. The priest put on a pantomime on one occasion, and it was so long that it was almost midnight when it concluded, half of the audience having left to catch the last buses at 11 p.m.!

It was said the reason the Sunday films ban lasted so long here was that the Sunday night stage shows were usually in aid of church funds! Many local dignitaries claimed credit for the eventual lifting of the ban, one prominent parish priest from St Patrick's claiming a discount from Tom English for a concert he organised on the grounds that it was he who had got the ban lifted!

The great social occasions in the Savoy were the symphony concerts by the Radio Eireann Symphony Orchestra (later RTE) where luminaries, booked for the dress circle, arrived dressed to the nines in formal evening wear. In Hollywood film premiere fashion, many of the ordinary citizens flocked to the doors of the cinema to see the style of the local glitterati, particularly the fur coats and the evening frocks.

Housewives, bedecked with their scarves, and their bicycles propped up outside the cinema, watched critically as the leaders of the city's social scene passed in, led by patrons such as Martin McGuire. Many witty and sometimes sarcastic comments were invariably passed.

One outstanding oratorio performance, of which I was lucky to have been a participant with the Limerick Choral Union in the mid-1960's, was of Beethoven's *Missa Solemnis*, with the legendary Tibor Paul conducting the RTE Symphony Orchestra, and Bernadette Greavy and Frank Patterson solists.

Many world-famous orchestras performed down the years, including the ever-popular Halle, under the famous Sir John Barbaroli. One memorable performance was by the Vienna Symphony State Orchestra which could have had disastrous consequences only for the intervention of Tom English, manager at the time.

Tom listened enthralled at the rehearsal as the orchestra swept through that gem of all waltzes, *The Blue Danube* and other immortal Strauss waltzes. The conductor then took the musicians through the national anthem, but to Tom's horror it was *God Save the Queen* they were playing! He called stage manager Alec O'Farrell who rushed up to the manager of the orchestra to point out the enormity of the mistake, but was told the orchestra had played Belfast the night before and it being the same country, did not *God Save the Queen* apply here as well! He was quickly informed it did not.

Tom was now in a fierce dilemma. With just a few copies of *Amrhan na bhFiann* available from Savin's Music Shop, and the advent of copying machines a thing of the future, where was he going to find copies for the orchestra? Local musician Tadhg Smalle came to the rescue, and with some help, copied by hand the required amount and saved the day.

Joe Malone, in 1947, with the Savoy girls

Tom recalled an epic journey a Wexfordman made to hear the orchestra. "He cycled all the way from Wexford but of course the concert had been well booked out. We took pity on him and we left him into the operation box to hear the concert."

The early 1960's saw some superb performances by the Limerick Choral and Operatic Society which included *Lucia di Lammermoor, Tosca, El Trovatore* and many more. Star tenor Stuart Burrows was one of the more memorable guests. In an era of great local talent, there were many outstanding performances from our own artistes as well. These operas gave great pleasure to local musical lovers and beyond, before the era sadly petered out in the middle of the decade mainly due to financial constraints and the advent of the great bugbear of live entertainment, i.e., television.

Most of the legendary Irish comedians were regular performers in the Savoy. Jimmy O'Dea was a great favourite, but in a highly conservative city, some of his jokes, completely harmless by today's standards, were regarded as smutty. It was said that he often threw a few of these sly jokes that only those in the front rows heard, which sent them into convulsions. Their infectious laughter set the tone for the show, and Jimmy and cast had them eating out of their hands for the rest of the night.

Sadly for Jimmy, one of his shows was denounced from the pulpit at a meeting of the Arch Confraternity in the Redemptorists. The show was described by the preacher as being vulgar, with double meaning jokes, and should not be supported. In this day and age, such denunciation would swell audiences, but in an era of religious compliance, there was a noticeable fall-off in attendances, and eventually Jimmy transferred to the City Theatre. He was later credited with describing Limerick as a city of piety and shiety, an unendearing term which usually is attributed to Brendan Behan.

Local character Robby Lawlor sued Jimmy on one memorable occasion for defamation. As in the fashion of the time, the comedian slipped the names of local characters into the script, and Robby was a favourite of his. An example was when the comedian was invoking names of the saints in a *Riders to the Sea* type of skit on the Abbey Theatre he'd include Robby's name on the list. On another occasion he asked what was the difference between Robby and a lift, the answer being that the lift would take you up but Robby would leave you down! The local, a well known trainer of greyhounds and the Limerick hurling team, and distinctive in his jodphurs, had enough and he brought the comedian to court. The judge found in favour of Robby who got something in the region of £25 damages.

Like many comedians, O'Dea could be cynical and officious and even his side-kick, Maureen Potter, was required to call him Mr. O'Dea. Cecil Sheridan was another great artist in the O'Dea stable and playing the Savoy to very small audiences in the middle of a heat wave was heard to remark that even if they put on the Last Supper with the original cast they wouldn't have filled the hall!

Jack Cruise was also a great favourite, invariably being booked out, and many a local man harboured secret desires for his star attraction, the talented and beautiful soprano, Patricia Cahill. Jack himself did a stint as manager of the Savoy.

Not all shows took off, one particular flop being Paddy Crosbie and his *School Around the Corner*. It was taken off after a week after some very poor houses, despite filling the Metropole in Dublin for a month.

One of the great successes of the cinema complex was the upstairs restaurant which was the eating place in the city in it prime, with Johnny McMahon providing ballroom dancing with his band. The snack bar down stairs attracted a less demanding clientele, where you could find anyone from a docker to a solicitor looking for a quick bite. For those on the tear on Sundays, the bar's famous tripe and mash proved a great antidote to the copious amount of pints quaffed during the day's excursions.

Earl Connolly, prime entertainer writer with the *Leader* for many years, had associations with the Savoy going back to its early days. He has recorded many great memories which included the thrill of hearing Robeson, Kreisler and McCormack, the Carl Rosa opera company, The Abbey Players, Mac Liammoir, and many more, and of course the great classic films like *Gone with the Wind*.

"For such blockbusters, there would be queues outside the Savoy for hours at a time. In those days performances were continuous," Earl recalled. Which meant of course that you could walk into the middle of the film, see out the finish, and wait on for the start!

Earl recalled the great stature of the managers down the years: Jimmy Sheil, "Uncle" Cliff Marsden, Norman Metcalfe, Jack Cruise, Jack Nordell (with film star looks, later found floating on the River Thames, apparently murdered), Tom English (appearance of being easy-going but astute and knowledgeable), Maurice Johnston and the last, John Likely.

The O'Farrell family will always be associated with the Savoy, Alec, stage manager, whom Tom English described as being indispensable to him; his brother Tommy and sister Nancy, were part of the cinema ethos for many years. Tom recalls some of the staff who worked under him. "They were a great bunch, with Michael Ryan as chief usher, a thorough gentlemen, and before him, Jim Ryan. In the restaurant May Bermingham was an institution and clients were willing to wait a half hour for one of her tables."

Tom recalled other staff who included projectionist Jim Carter, there from the beginning, with Dick Murphy, Paddy Moran, and Paddy Guerin. Cashiers were Fizzie O'Riordan from Bengal Terrace, and May Kiely, Thomas Street.

"When our usherettes lined up it was like a mannequin parade with the likes of Eileen Kelleher, Nancy O'Farrell, Celine Horrigan, Gerry Byrnes, Mollie Barrington, Noreen Flanagan, Miss Wallace, Miss Finn. In the snack bar Bridget Mullan reigned supreme, and you were barred from using unseemly language. Others I recall there were Madge Hinchey and Mrs. Walsh, with Mickey Hehir the chief chef. Benny Franklin, was electrician, who had the task of checking the cinema's temperature every four hours, and a night watchman was a great character called Pat O'Shea from around Ellen Street who never stopped singing.

"Cliff Marsden was a most colourful manager, and got the appellation Uncle Cliff when he ran children's shows. I was his assistant when he died in Barrington's in 1954, and as he had no relations, boss Louis Elliman gave me the job of making funeral arrangement which included buying a habit in Todds to lay Cliff out." Tom, who came from Waterford, was only twenty-two when he took over from Cliff.

Of all the industrial strikes that took place in Limerick over the years, few could compare to that of the acrimonious cinema dispute that started on Monday, October 29, 1951. Cinema proprietors offered to settle on an individual basis but this was rejected by the unions. The strike lasted almost seven months, dragging on into May, 1952, despite the intervention of Mayor Stevie Coughlan and other prominent citizens. With strike money eventually drying up, and despite collections to alleviate the suffering of the workers and their families, Savoy and other cinema employees were practically on the bread line before the dispute was settled. For a cinema mad public in a pre TV era, it was also a frustrating time, and those few possessed with cars were often pressed into service to transport fans to neighbouring towns to see their favourite films and stars.

Tom English recalled that traumatic time: "It was a bitter dispute, with two particular local cinema proprietors being intransigent in negotiations. There were many meetings with prominent local politicians mediating, but all broke down. Eventually a Franciscan priest brokered an agreement, but the cinema proprietors came out on top. The male workers eventually had to settle for eight shillings a week (they were looking for £1) with the women doing a little better, getting less than half of their claim, 4/6d. I think it was."

Tom recalled the great Pioneer Total Abstinence Rallies on Sunday afternoons with the suave and incomparable Conn Shanahan as MC. "They came from every corner in the county and were entertained by many great artistes, visiting and local."

The former manager remembered one of those concerts, put on for the schools, after which a Jesuit, Fr. Higgins, asked a pertinent question. "How do you manage to control the youngsters in the front stalls during the cinema matinees? Many of them would be from Corporation schemes wouldn't they?"

Tom stuck him to the ground.

"As a matter of fact, Father, it is the youngsters in the in the balcony seats that give us all the trouble."

"And where would they be from now," asked the priest.

"They would all be pupils from your own Crescent College, and Laurel Hill."

Aghast, Fr. Higgins departed, arriving back post haste with another well known Jesuit, Fr. Bates.'

"Can you name names of these Crescent boys that are giving you trouble," asked Fr. Bates.

"Certainly," said Tom, listing out several of the trouble makers.

The culprits were barred from further attendance in the Savoy.

"Several of those young blackguards are now leading businessmen in the city, and I count them amongst my friends," Tom recalled with a laugh.

Another feic maker who

was put on the barred list was Dickie Harris, as we knew him. "He would get up to all sort of antics during the films," recalled Grace (O'Malley) Cantillon. "He had such a presence even at that early age that his arrival in the cinema invariably caused a stir."

Richard had the last laugh. He got a standing ovation when the world premiere of his film, *Bloomfield*, was staged at the cinema from which he was barred in his younger days. Another great local character, avid Limerick F.C. supporter Gerry O'Brien, used cause great amusement if his favourites were being shown in cup action on the newsreels. He would stand up and invariably abuse the referee the same as if he was in the Markets Field.

Lying on a level with the docks, the cinema was flooded on several occasions during extreme weather

SAVOY CINEMA AND RESTAURANT LIMERICK

TO-DAY: CONTINUOUS FROM 2.30 TO 11 P.M. FULL OPENING PROGRAMME.

"BREWSTER'S MILLIONS"

With JACK BUCHANAN and LILI DAMITA. A Rollicking Comedy from the Famous Stage Play.
SHOWING AT 3.17, 5.25, 7.33 AND 9.41.

| MUSICAL MOOD No. 1. | MICKEY'S KANGAROO. | TORTOISE AND HARE. | PATHE GAZETTE. |
| A Musical Travel Film of Irish Beauty. | Mickey Mouse in a Clever Screen Cartoon. | A Colour Silly Symphony. | NEWS FEATURE. |

ALBAN CHAMBERS, Mus.B., F.R.C.O., AT THE MAGNIFICENT SAVOY ORGAN.

conditions, the water flowing into the stalls from Henry Street. During the great industrial upheavals of the 1970's and 1980's, it was often found necessary to cut programmes short due to E.S.B. disputes, deadlines of 10 pm having to be adhered to.

"The advent of television in 1961 was the first peal of the death knell of the great cinemas like the Savoy,' Tom English claimed. "Average attendances before the opening of Telefis Eireann were 14,000 to 16,000 a week. In a short time, this had dropped to 10,000 and then it was down to 8,000 when I left. This showed the catastrophic effect of the new medium on cinema attendances."

Amazingly, the Savoy, even in its heyday, was never a viable proposition according to Tom. "It was modelled on the great West End theatres in London. The overheads were terrific, with a huge pay bill. There were four usherettes, six cloakroom attendants, twelve full time cleaners, four page boys, even a full time plumber and electrician with their assistants. It was a great thing to get a job in the Savoy and there was invariably a queue when vacancies occurred. Prominent citizens such as Stevie Coughlan and Tadhg Smalle were often approached to use their influence to get people jobs there.'

Joe Coleman, formerly of Thomondgate, went to work in the Savoy as a lounge boy in the bar in 1972, graduating to the projection room where he worked with the late Jimmy Carter and Pat O'Brien, and also, amongst others, Dick Murphy, Benny Franklin, Eddie Connery, Christy O'Neill, Alec and Tommy O'Farrell, Frank Sarsfield, Tom Marsden, and John Collopy.

He was there when the sad news came through that after forty years of continuous showings, the cinema era was to end in 1975. "It was television that finished it," claimed Joe. "The company claimed they were making more money in the sweet shop than from the films."

Manager John Likely blamed bingo and TV as the cause of the closure. "When RTE was off the air on New Year's Eve we had over 800 admissions in the cinema, whereas on the two previous nights we had less than 200." It was estimated that the cinema could be bought for a sum in the region of £300,000.

With the cinema due to close at the end of January, 1975, many appeals were made to keep the venue open. John Likely pleaded with the Corporation and Arts Council to come together and save what he claimed could be a profitable complex. Comedian Jack Cruise, a former manager and hugely popular here, made an emotional appeal to the people of Limerick not to leave the cinema close: "If the Savoy goes, part of Limerick will go too."

It was all in vain. *Closure a tragedy for Limerick* was the headline in the *Leader* on February 1st, 1975, as the cinema closed its doors, forty years after they first opened. It was like a death in the family for many Limerick people.

To Jack Cruise fell the dubious honour of presenting the last show of that era with the aptly named "Farewell Cruise." John O'Shaughnessy, writing in the Leader,

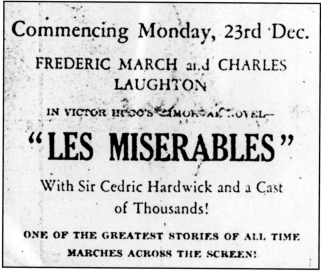

Commencing Monday, 23rd Dec.

FREDERIC MARCH and CHARLES LAUGHTON

IN VICTOR HUGO'S IMMORTAL NOVEL

"LES MISERABLES"

With Sir Cedric Hardwick and a Cast of Thousands!

ONE OF THE GREATEST STORIES OF ALL TIME MARCHES ACROSS THE SCREEN!

Film showing Christmas week 1935

was not pleased with the production, however, and wrote that it was anything but a fitting farewell to what he described as the Palace of Variety. "It was a show of bits and pieces, and it looked as if the cast had been assembled in a few hours," he wrote. He was pleased though with the performances of local artistes Kay Condron and Edmund Browne.

Ten months later, however, there was joy, when the Savoy got a reprieve. Its eventual saviour was Brendan Murray whose impresario skills brought many great acts to the venue. Famous artistes who performed in the 1970's and 1980's included singer Tom Jones, comedian Dick Emery, who played to 3,000 patrons in a double evening performance. Many patrons were disappointed, however, at the fare on offer by the English comedian.

The Dubliners were another legendary group who played but who on one famous occasion failed to turn up. The reason: they got caught up in the funeral of the Clare traditional musician Willie Clancy. Patrons were eventually reimbursed.

The Savoy was to remain open for another thirteen years, with many memorable stage performances being performed. These included a golden era of local entertainment with the staging of the Tops of the Town variety show competitions. Some of the early productions were put on by such as the Insurances, Burlington, Ferenka, etc. "These were a lot less spectacular than shows which were to follow, which often cost up to £10,000 to produce," recalled Joe Coleman.

Other local talent also burgeoned with the best of the highly successful Siamsa finals. These shows proved hugely popular and gave great entertainment, as

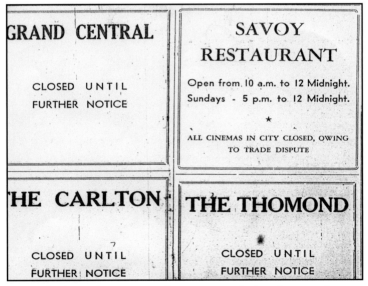

Blank Leader cinema advertisements during the marathon cinema strike, 1951/52

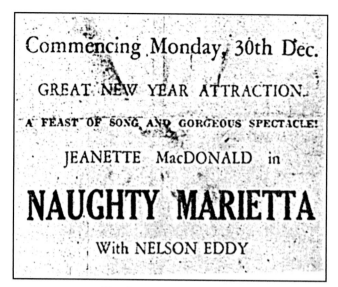

New Year's attraction 1935

exemplified by full houses. For the participants, also, it was a great era of social interaction, and many friendships were forged that have lasted to this day. Sadly, changing mores and deference to the Celtic Tiger have put paid to these very worthwhile social activities enjoyed by parish groups, and the great losers are the younger generation.

Tragically, Brendan Murray died suddenly after years of endeavour trying to keep the grand old venue open, and bereft of a guiding light, the writing was now on the wall for the Savoy. The final curtain came in the spring of 1988.

There was great sadness amongst the older generation when the great Savoy era, of "pictures" and unsurpassed stage entertainment, finally came to an end. According to Broad Street's Frankie Bourke, the last show to be staged there was a Barra O Tuama operatic concert and fittingly, one of the great musical institutions of the city played in the concert, i.e., the Boherbuoy Band.

Melancholy we watched as the bulldozers levelled the familiar edifice that for half a century was the hub of the great entertainment of the city and its environs. It was as if it was trying to hold on, as the demolishers found it tough going trying to cut through the mass concrete and pre-war steel that doggedly refused to budge. "Special cutting equipment had to be brought in from abroad," Joe Coleman remembers.

Eventually it was levelled and the new building ushered in the multiplex cinema era, complete with restaurant, bar and bowling alley. That lasted just fourteen years and the bulldozers returned for the second time in 2005 to put in train the third phase of this storied site. The city centre was now bereft of a cinema that once boasted six: the Athenaeum (later Royal) Coliseum, Carlton, Grand Central, Lyric, Savoy.

While Bedford Row is being remodelled and pedestrianised, an irreplaceable landmark is gone forever with the demise of the Savoy. Thankfully, such as the L.I.T. the U.L. concert halls have filled the void as regards major stage venues, but the Savoy will always hold a special place in the memory of the people of Limerick.

In the projection box, 1974, were Anthony Coleman, Jimmy Carter (R.I.P.), chief operator, and Joe Coleman.

The end . . . . the last remnants of the Savoy come tumbling down in 1989.

The story of Park Bridge

DOZENS of curious St. Mary's parishioners crowd Park Bridge in the early 1920's gazing at a lorry transporting flour from Corbally Mill which went out of control, crashed through a parapet, and was within a foot or two from toppling into the river. Park Bridge (replaced by O'Dwyer Bridge in 1931), according to Lenihan in his history, was built in 1798 by the Monsell family, major land owners in the Corbally area.

A curious clause in all of the leases of Corbally tenants stated that they would have an abatement of £3 per acre in the rental of their lands should Park Bridge at any time go out of repair. The rents were raised when the bridge was erected, and the landlord was obliged to keep the bridge in repair.

The rental of lands in Corbally in mid-19th century was £16 16s 6d an acre. With the passing of the Athlunkard Bridge Act in 1825, Park Bridge ceased to be a private bridge, and the roadway over it came under the jurisdiction of the Athlunkard Bridge Commissioners, who thus became responsible for its maintenance.

While both the Park and O'Dwyer Bridges were located roughly in the same position at the end of Athlunkard Street, Park Bridge veered to the right and connected with the road outside Healy's House. The remains of an old wall near Healy's, still extant, shows where the bridge ended. Another reminder of the old bridge can be seen in Cowhey's pub in the Sandmall in the form of an old oak bollard which was a strut for the pedestrian walkway across the Abbey River while the old bridge was being demolished and the new structure under construction.

The building in the background of the above photograph is that of the ruins of the old Lock Mills on the canal, which was demolished in the 1940's. Its location in the photograph is puzzling, the cause of which is probably the reversal of the negative.

When a child played with it's dying mother

St. John's Hospital towards the end of the 19th century.

FOR the vast majority of the citizens of Limerick, the second half of the 1840's was a time of great tribulation. Famine and disease stalked the streets as thousands of starving natives of the county, and Clare, poured into the city looking for relief. Compliantly these famine victims waited in droves outside the Union, or City Home (now St Camillus) waiting for admittance, with many of them dying at its gates. It has been recorded that so dense was the crowd that the gates could not be opened and the workforce of the Union had to scale the walls with ladders in an effort to gain admittance to their place of employment.

While the worst excesses of the famine began to abate towards the end of the decade, a new and terrible development now arose in the city As the result of the years of starvation, unhygienic conditions, particularly the foul water supply, a devastating cholera epidemic broke out 1849. The plague did not discern between young and old, rich or poor, and in its wake left countless dead.

Indeed, so multiple were the coffins being taken from Barrington's Hospital that the residents on the opposite side of the Abbey River, in the then upmarket Assembly Mall (Charlotte Quay) objected to the grisly sight. The hospital authorities complied to the objections, deciding to remove the coffins via a side entrance into Mary Street, the outline of which can still be seen on the walls.

Witnesses to the dreadful plague were the Sisters of Mercy from St. Mary's Convent and their accounts, recorded in their annals, paint an appalling picture. In the overcrowded wards of St John's Hospital the disease was so virulent that on their rounds, when returning to patients they had given drinks of water a short interval before, the sisters found they had expired. And in that short interval, the corpses had been removed and other victims put in place in the bed.

Some of Sisters were wonderful versifiers, none more so than Mother Mary Vincent, who described the scene at Barrington's as the nuns took up duty shortly after the outbreak of the plague:

Yes! We are ready, lead us on
To work ere this our day is gone.
You now must pass two days from this
To see a sight 'twere worth to miss–
The hour is one -- the day is fine
Beds packed up since half past nine
With all their needful laid in state
On a donkey's cart outside the gate,
In order thus to be conveyed
And on their stretchers neatly made
In that abode you know full well
I mean St, Mary's Hospital (Barrington's)
And not alone to that, don't frown,
But one beyond the Englishtown (St John's)
Eight Sisters stand within the hall,
In cloaks and bonnets – shoes on all,*
With hearts of zeal and pockets light,
You never before saw such a sight.
In one hour after take a view,
You see them stepping two by two
Through the streets and in the doors
Of those haunts I speak of just before.
Oh! I could wish for just one hour
For poet's brains or any power
The scenes they witnessed to describe
That you some notion may imbibe
Of all they did and had to do.

(*In mid 19th century, it was quite normal to see women of common class going barefoot, and urchins following the Sisters of Mercy on their first appearance in Killarney, shouted, "there they go, shoes on all").

The Sisters did heroic work during the duration of the epidemic (and in previous epidemics) both in their visitations to hovels and taking up residence in both Barrington's and St John's so that they could be on hand to minister to the victims. They had huge problems to confront, some of the beds being occupied by more than one patient. This further exacerbated the desperate situation due to the fact the disease had varying effects: one victim burning with heat, another intensively cold, some insensible and others unable to continue for a minute in the same posture.

The first night the Sisters spent in St. John's, nineteen persons died. Add the fatalities taking place in Barrington's Hospital and in hovels throughout the city, the enormity of the epidemic can be appreciated. One of the most poignant stories emanating from those terrible weeks in Lent occurred in St John's and concerned a two-year-old child, Mary Burke, who was described in the annals as being beautiful. Though she knew she was dying, Mary's mother insisted on nursing her child to the end and when she eventually succumbed. Mary, still playing with her, had to be prised away from the corpse.

Now orphaned, the child was taken to the House of Mercy in St Mary's to be cared for and was occasionally brought in to amuse the Sisters at recreation. According to the annals, "the poor child, imbibed with the seeds of disease, so pined away and in a few months she went unstained by sin to eternal glory."

When victims were coffined, even their families were afraid to open the lid to have a last look at their loved ones in case of catching the dreaded plague. One poor man, when told that his wife had died, collected her coffin, buried her and shortly afterwards was astonished to be informed that his wife was not dead, and had recovered in St John's, but had no clothes to go home. "It cannot be," he said, "I am after burying my poor Peggy."

Hurrying to the hospital, he found that indeed a dreadful mistake had been made and his real wife was alive and waiting to go home. Her garments were sent for and she was brought home in great triumph to the joy of her daughters. The poor man's elation, however, was highly tempered by the fact that he had spent a good sum on the funeral of a corpse which had been mistaken for his wife.

Another poignant story from the annals of the Sisters was about a young boy, who on the point of death, was anointed by Rev. Fr. George Butler, afterwards Bishop, who also heard his last confession. Moving away, the boy called him and bawled for the whole ward to hear: "Oh Your Reverence, I forgot to tell you I stole a pair of boots." The nuns could but turn away in a moment of amusement.

Contemporary reports brought the horrors of the epidemic home. During the worst excesses of the plague, the corpses were piled high in the dead-houses (mortuaries) and the late Kevin Hannan recorded an authenticated account of a mother taking her son from such a pile and nursing him back to health.

The *Limerick Chronicle* reported that two boys were bringing ten corpses every day to Killalee graveyard and as they were unable to bury them there, the dogs were devouring the corpses. Historian Ernest Bennis has recorded that members of his family in William Street used to hear the dead-cart going round in the mornings, with the driver calling out "any dead here, any dead here" with the bodies being buried in a great pit with quick-lime in the old Killeen Cemetery in Corbally, near the entrance to the old Bishop's Palace in the Mill Road, now St Munchin's College.

Mother Vincent, writing to a nun in Mallow,

Sr. M. Philomena Potter's grave in St. Mary's Convent.

graphically recaptures the terrible suffering she witnessed during the outbreak of the cholera:
And ever when we watched the dying
Many more were loudly crying:
Oh, the cramps, I have a score
Sisters, won't you rub ashtore?
Mother of Mercy, Mother dear,

One drop of water bring me here
To cool my heart that's hotly burning,
My stomach cure that's hourly turning
And raise them to my children dear,
Their wretched hearths and homes to cheer.

A dying Welshman was so impressed by the charitable work of the Sisters in St. John's that he converted to Catholicism near the end. Pointing out a Mother M. McNamara, he stated: "I'll be of the religion of that tall woman. It must be good, she works so hard, and I heard she gets no pay."

It was inevitable that some of the Sisters would succumb to the disease and Sister Mary Philomena Potter died on April 19, 1849, following heroic and non-stop work with the cholera patients in Barrington's and St. John's.

The Grand Jury, at its assembly in Limerick at the end of the year, passed a resolution lauding the work of the Sisters:

That the highest praise is deserved by the Sisters of Mercy in this city for their ceaseless exertions in the cause of charity and more especially during the prevalence of cholera and that the thanks of the Grand Jury are hereby given them.

Despite the terrible calamity taking place all round them, the nuns did not lose their sense of humour. To help alleviate the suffering of victims, hot punch (called the "cure", consisting of hot water, sugar and port wine concocted by the foundress, Mother McAuley in Dublin) was prescribed and the Sisters gained a reputation of making as good a glass of the spirit as could be found in the city. This was the cause of much amusement amongst them. Mother Vincent wrote of two patients discussing the quality of the punch:

One night about the hour of eight
The belles dames held a tete a tete.
'Tis true they were not very bad
The sickness though they lately had,
Nor did they think a soul was near

Their little confab then to hear;
One said, "Oh, Kitty did you taste
A drop of what the nun's tin graced?
'Twas strong and sweet and seemed quite rough,
You ne'er before drank better stuff."
"Yes," Kitty answered, "Spite of Fate
They make good punch at any rate."–
You see, dear Sister, how our name
Has risen to a brilliant flame
That sheds its light both far and near.
Not far away a listener sat*
And one who often wears a hat–
Employed in giving consolation
To someone sunk in desolation.
You may be sure it passed him not
But round the town it quickly shot,
And we have got what none could dream–
For MAKING PUNCH – a noted name.

(*The listener was Rev. Fr. Casey, C.C., St John's, appointed P.P. in St Mary's in 1871 on the death of Dr. Michael Fitzgerald).

The Great Exhibition of 1906: questions raised in the Commons

A view of the impressive entrance to the Munster and Connacht Great Exhibtion, held in the Haymarket, Cathedral Place, in the summer of 1906.

WHEN Cork held its famous Great Exhibition in 1902 (eulogised in the song *The Bold Thady Quill*), it was decided that anything Cork could do Limerick could do better. So the idea of the Great Munster and Connacht Exhibition was born, and came to fruition when it was opened by the Lord Lieutenant, the Earl of Aberdeen, in July, 1906.

Held in the grounds of the Haymarket in Cathedral Place, most local industries, including the four bacon factories, Shaw's, Denny's, Matterson's, O'Mara's, had stands and firms from all over Munster and Connacht exhibited.

Many cultural events took place in a specially erected hall, which included choir and band recitals, and

The Lord Lieutenant of Ireland, the Earl of Aberdeen, opened the Great Munster and Connacht Exhibition in Limerick in 1906. His Majesty King Edward VII's representative in Ireland, he led a grand procession through the main streets, his open carriage drawn by two white horses. The cortege paused to let the populace have a look at the main intersection of the city where to the right can be seen McBirney's drapery emporium, taken over by Roche's Stores and burned to the ground in a disastrous fire in 1948, and replaced by the present building. In the centre is E. G. Fitt grocery shop, and Nestor's, who moved across the road in later years.

Irish cultural events. One of the attractions was the Shilissima Band, a Japanese Ladies' Orchestra, and the participation of many of the great military bands created great atmosphere. These included the 87th Royal Irish Fusiliers known as the Faugh-a-Ballaghs; Royal Irish Rifles, 2nd Royal Munster Fusiliers. A grand tattoo saw eight bands taking part including the Gordon Highlanders doing their famous sword dances.

In an era of great industrial depression the exhibition was a call to arms for a great manufacturing revival, with Edward Thomas O'Dwyer, Bishop of Limerick, being in the forefront of the renewal. He exhorted priests to be the leaders in this movement and P.P.'s all over the country organised trains which brought thousands of viewers to the exhibition. An estimated quarter of a million attended the exhibition, which went on right through to October

Many lived in squalor at that time, and one of the attractions of the exhibition was "showhouses" of labourers' cottages with demonstrations in household management and domestic economy. Farming and produce also played an important part with the Limerick Agricultural and Horticultural Society being formed as an outcome of the exhibition.

Admission to the exhibition was 6d and towards the end this was reduced to three-pence. A letter to the Leader claimed that there were many thousands of people in the city who could not even afford this reduced admission of truppence and called for an admission free day each week.

The Lord Lieutenant, the Earl of Aberdeen, accompanied by Lady Aberdeen, opened the exhibition amidst great pomp. They were introduced by the Mayor, Ald. Michael Joyce, M.P. Lady Aberdeen made several purchases in the Cannocks stand, the receipt of which the firm used in advertising afterwards.

Straight away controversy surrounded the Exhibition. The fact that the Union Jack was not flown got widespread publicity and Captain Craig of the

A model showing a dress made in Limerick.

Orange Order, raising the matter in the House of Commons, looked for support for a resolution "that Lord Aberdeen shall not in future take part in public functions when resolutions against the use of the British flag have been passed."

In the discussions that followed, the Mayor, Ald. Joyce, who was M.P. for Limerick, challenged the motion, asking what the English flag had got to do with an Irish exhibition. Mr. Bryce, chief secretary, said the Cabinet, himself and the country had perfect confidence in the high sense of duty, judgment and tact of the Lord Lieutenant, adding "I regret any member of the House should put such a question."

Even in those far off days poor Limerick was denigrated and uproar followed when at a meeting of the Cork Corporation the poor state of that city's municipal flag was discussed and Sir Abraham Sutton stated "that

The Irish Ladies Choir performing at the exhibition.

for a duster I would send it up to the Limerick Exhibition as a present from Cork, or something like that. It is a disreputable looking thing."

Exhibition secretary E. Travers wrote of the "gross insult" afforded the organisers and the citizens of Limerick and called for an unreserved apology from Sir Abraham.

The slur reverberated even to Tipperary where at the Board of Guardians meeting members spoke of the insult to Limerick with several speaking against awarding the coal tender to His Lordship's firm. Soon after the incident, however, Sir Abraham apologised profusely saying that he meant no slur on Limerick, and

that he was misunderstood. "I have too much regard for the city and people of Limerick to be capable of offending them in any way whatever."

Sadly, while the Exhibition was voted a great success, the aftermath ended in tears and recriminations (the curse of St. Munchin raising its ugly head again?) The balance sheet showed a working loss of £3,000, a huge amount then, which meant that those who went as guarantors were having to make up the deficit. It was stated that many of them could not afford the loss, no-one foreseeing that they would be called on to cough up.

At a consequent meeting the Mayor, backed by Ald. Stephen O'Mara, rounded on the Limerick Leader stating "for months past it did its level best against the exhibition and he blamed only one man for that - and he is not a Limerickman - and he now controls the Leader (he was referring to E. B. Duggan). They tried to cut our throats and at the same time took all the money it could from the Exhibition."

Ald. O'Mara, obviously on his pickey, waded in again, saying: "that from start to finish they were met by a few, mangey lousy fellows" (laughter), but immediately withdrew the remarks.

The *Leader* ran a weekly column containing comments on the Exhibition, mostly laudatory but sometimes critical. The newspaper had an ultra national outlook and criticised the fact that members of the R.I.C. and military bands were hired, "making it a tattoo for Tommies and a huge help to the recruiting sergeant." It also stated that there was not enough made of local and national talent.

In direct opposite, the loyalist organ the *Limerick Chronicle*, was critical of the lack of the loyalist "rags" and the insult to the King by not displaying the Union Jack. It also criticised the lack of military bands and R.I.C. (written before they were hired).

In a two-column editorial the Leader refuted the charges levelled against it, citing the huge amount of space it had afforded the exhibition. It defended criticism it had made by being in the best interests of the Exhibition. "An attempt has been made to make us scapegoats in the matter and we have been vindicated when the secretary in his final report never mentioned anything about the Leader. We believe the problem was that the Exhibition should have finished in August rather than October."

The huge financial loss was the subject of much debate for weeks afterwards, even in the National Press. It was stated that one of the prime reasons for the loss was that the Cork Exhibition, which showed a profit of £12,000, got "£27,000 as a grant against a measly £500 for Limerick"

The affairs of the Exhibition were put into the hands of a liquidator and the plight of the guarantors was again brought up, the claim being made that many of them could ill-afford to pay, "initially believing that they would never have been called upon for a penny." Some relief was afforded when it was announced, on the intervention of Lord Monteagle, that the Department of Agriculture would pay £500 against the deficit.

Settlements for full amounts were eventually made to all the creditors. Ironically, the first claimant at the Quarterly Sessions was the *Limerick Leader* who claimed £10 4s. for advertising.

(The above extracts were taken from a scrapbook of the Exhibition meticulously recorded by Dick Hartigan, (assistant secretary of the Exhibition), son of Patrick Hartigan, proprietor of the Royal George Hotel, which passed into the hands of Dick and his brother on the death of his father. Thanks to Richard Coughlan for the use of the scrapbook).

The gramophone was a novelty in 1906 and this newspaper cartoon shows country visitors at the exhibition listening intently to the new contraption.

Tales from the Congress

This magnificent triumphal arch graced the middle of a tree-lined Athlunkard Street to celebrate the Eucharistic Congress being held in Dublin in June, 1932. The archway, erected opposite the gate to the entrance of the church grounds, was modelled on the Emperor Constantine's grand memorial in Rome and was a source of great pride to St. Mary's parishioners. James A. O'Farrell and his son Martin, Athlunkard Street, played a major part in the construction of the archway. The splendid furniture in the vestry of St. Mary's Church is a testimony to the family's workmanship. Note at the end of the street the start of the old Park Bridge (replaced by the O'Dwyer bridge) which swept to the right and finished near Healy's house.

UNTIL THE visit of Pope John Paul II to Ireland in 1979, the Eucharistic Congress of 1932 was the greatest outpouring of religious fervour in the history of the country. It would be the rare Catholic household that would not have displayed in its windows, holy pictures, statutes, candles or flowers. Many triumphant archways like the one in Athlunkard Street (above) were erected throughout the city, and residents of streets and lanes vied with one another with displays of buntings and religious banners.

The Limerick Development Association set the lead, with the main streets being "magnificently decorated" as the *Leader* described it. Fr. Murray, director of the men's arch confraternity, made a tour of the city to inspect the decorations, and described them as splendid. "The people were deserving of all commendation," he said.

J.D.H., writing in the *Leader*, said "in most people's lifetime there is always some outstanding event that cannot be duplicated. In this instance it may be the greatest Congress the world has yet seen that will set its dominant seal on our experiences."

J.D.H. travelled by bus to Dublin on the Thursday "the roads being so excellent that it could hardly be said we were on a pilgrimage. Every house, hamlet, and town, brightened our journey with their tributes to the 'King of Kings.' Still in mid-week, they were everywhere busy putting the finishing touches to them in every form that taste and reverence suggested. There were some midland towns beautifully done, but who could resist a better look at the shrines that sparkled amongst the humbler quarters of old Limerick."

It was estimated that on the Sunday, June 19th, 8,000 Limerick people travelled by train to Dublin for the final day of the Congress in the Phoenix Park, where up to a million witnessed the impressive closing ceremony. Four special trains from Limerick carried members of the Arch Confraternity of the Holy Family and the women's confraternities of St. John's, St. Michael's and St. Mary's - "all that is best in the womanhood of Limerick" said the *Leader* report on Monday. Many more had left on Friday and Saturday. Also on board were the members of the Corporation who were met by the Mayor, Ald. P. J. Donnellan, on their arrival in the capital.

The members of the Confraternity, when they arrived in Phoenix Park, were allotted a prominent position near the high altar, "befitting the largest organised body of Catholic lay men in the world"

continued the report. Each man wore his confraternity medal and ribbon and they presented a "striking and most edifying sight."

As the banner of the Confraternity was unfurled, the *Leader* reporter waxed eloquent. "An inspiring manifestation of Limerick's undying loyalty to the Church – of Limerick militant," and then quoted the famous confraternity rallying hymn which he said came to one's lips: *Confraternity men to the fight, and raise up your banner on high; Jesus, Mary and Joseph in sight, in our battles their names be our cry.*

In many parts of the city on that day, touching scenes were witnessed as those unable to travel to Dublin listened into the radio. Few households would have owned radios at the time and the houses of those who did possess them were packed to overflowing. The listeners fell on their knees during the consecration of the Mass and later when the Papal Legate gave the Benediction. They joined in the responses to the Rosary and sang wholeheartedly the hymns.

In Clarina, the local correspondent was profuse in his thanks to the Ruttles of the Post Office for letting the people of the neighbourhood listen in to the broadcast. "Mr. and Mrs. Ruttle and Mr. Ivan Ruttle of the Post Office, Clarina, put their home and grounds at the disposal of the people and spared no effort in making them comfortable."

With such huge crowds travelling to Dublin, there was the inevitable tragedy. Timothy Enright of Ardagh, missing the train in Newcastle West, prevailed on a motor cyclist named Sullivan to travel to Ardagh to head off the train. On the journey, Enright was thrown from the bicycle, sustaining fatal injures, while Sullivan escaped with some bruises.

The Newcastle West cor. wrote that 400 pilgrims travelled on the special train, happy in the thought that they would be attending the greatest religious function which Ireland had ever seen. "But when the great event was over, and the trek to the railway station began, it

Tree-lined Island Road in St. Mary's decorated during the Congress.

was then only that one realised the terror of a crowd, and what a desperate effort was needed to secure being taken on the homeward bound train. Many had to stand all the way home. It was seven a.m. on Monday morning before the train arrived home."

It could have been worse. The special train from Killaloe with 200 pilgrims did not arrive home until 11 a.m. on the Monday morning. The correspondent delivered a missive in his Notes: "The Eucharistic Congress has come and gone, but the solemn grandeur of it, its majesty and great spiritual awakening live on in the hearts of our people for years to come. It is

something to remember when nations are warring with each other, contending endless strife to wrest the petty power which each imagines the other to hold. The strength and unity of our Holy Church throughout nations and all ages stand out as an example to those whose only ambition is the possession of property and have an elastic conscience to the manner in which their selfish goals are gained."

Then there were those who cycled all the way to Dublin for the Congress. These included 70 year old Maurice Dillane from Bottomstown, Knocklong. His bicycle was mentioned in a court case a few years later

142

when State Solicitor Mr. Power, questioned Dillane about a claim he made for a bicycle (worth £10) commandeered by the I.R.A. during the Troubles.

"Was that the bicycle you used when cycling to the Eucharistic Congress?" the State Solicitor enquired, obviously trying to trip up the plaintiff.

Dillane: "No."

When hearing the claimant was seventy when he cycled to the Congress, Judge McElligott was highly impressed and awarded Dillane £8 10s.

An abiding memory of the Congress was of Count John McCormack, in his full papal uniform, singing the *Panis Angelicus* during the dispensation of Holy Communion during the High Mass. There is a story told that a character from St. Francis Abbey called Hadah Sweeney was so transported by the voice of McCormack that he famously uttered: "I'd give a pound to be able to sing like him!"

The early part of the 20th century was a great era of punning and many of the banners erected in the city for the Congress were reputed to have borne the following legends:

Feed my lambs, feed my sheep (butcher's stall)
We pledge our souls to thee oh Lord (pawnbrokers)
My God and my all (shoemaker shop)
Happy we who thus united (banner connecting pawnbrokers in Broad Street)
Give us this day our daily bread (baker's shop)
Come to our aid Oh Lord when our battles are nigh (outside tinker's caravan).

A Co. Limerick born priest, Rev. P. J. Carroll, of Croagh, Rathkeale, covered the Congress for the prominent American Catholic magazine, *The Ave Maria*. He wrote that during the week-long ceremonies the weather was glorious; the third week of brightness and warmth that had not been experienced here for twelve years. "So say the seanachies who have a memory of wars, stories and the weather," he wrote.

Anxious to interview some of the dignitaries attending a ceremony at the Pro-Cathedral, Fr. Carroll approached two priests who pointed out Count John McCormack sitting just a few seats away. "Well, right before you is Count John McCormack. He should make a headliner for your 'Ave Maria'," one the priests said.

Approaching the famous tenor, Fr. Carroll finds out that "he is a human, warm man, but I suspect (sadly) he has never heard of me. He is due to sing the *Panis Angelicus* at the High Mass in the Phoenix Park and admits he is nervous about it."

"Any artist should feel a bit nervous – it is a compliment to his hearers," said McCormack. "A priest should always experience a certain nervousness before he preaches. It shows consideration for his congregation."

Fr. Carroll added the McCormack was anxious that he should be addressed as Count, a title bestowed on him by the Sovereign Pontiff, and an honour of which he feels very proud.

The priest made some shrewd observations as the Government Cabinet took their places in the Cathedral. He described the president (*sic*) Eamon de Valera, as having an ascetic face, "his severe formal dress does not escape you. He might well be set down as a somewhat mature man pursuing his studies in some ecclesiastical seminary, home now for his holidays. He makes a full genuflection, kneels on the priedieu and forgets seemingly clerical and lay officialdom.

"Back of the President is Major General Brennan, Chief of Army staff, in whose keeping Mr. de Valera was once confined as prisoner of war during the 'Troubles.' This surely illustrates the irony of politics, or of war if you will have it that way.

"Lord Mayor Byrne of Dublin seems a small man as he marches by, gorgeous in his official robe and chain, and sits with his official family not far behind Mr. Cosgrave.

"You see them all: de Valera, Cosgrave, Sean Kelly, James Geoghegan, J. P. Ryan, Finlan Lynch, P.

McGilligan, and it does not escape you that practically every one of them was marked and tabulated for death by the British government during the revolution which began in 1916. They are all so peaceful now and so silent you wonder how much would be required to stir them again. And Cosgrave seems so retreating, so meek; de Valera so detached, so sad-faced, so absorbed in some other world beyond this."

The Windmill, with the docks in the background, played its part.